"The text in this book is
authenticity. Real-life experiences of surviving the world, being hurt in the process, and rising from the ashes to improve the lives of others on a similar journey have power! The hurdles encountered, as well as an old set of systems that were not built for us, are revealed by the unyielding truth conveyed in each chapter of this book."

Prince Marshall
Assistant Superintendent of Student and Family Support Services I Madera Unified School District

---

"I was totally immersed in Felipe's story, and not solely because of my empathetic heart. I was entranced by his ability to reach me and teach me that life is not without promise if you dare to look back to learn and commit to looking forward to succeeding."

Gordon Jackson
Vice President, Prevention Education
3Strands Global Foundation

"There is much to admire about the journey that is Dr. Mercado. The openness with which he describes the struggles he faced should be a lesson-learned for anyone who sees little hope for their future."

Dr. Ken Magdaleno
Founder/President/CEO
Center for Leadership, Equity, and Research (CLEAR)

"A Journey To Compassion: Learning to Stand Firm in the Face of Pain, brings a sense of reflection that every human has experienced pain and illuminates a path of turning this trauma we can carry into authenticity and compassion. This book will provide insight into creating mindfulness for yourself, being non-judgmental, and supporting the idea that everyone has experienced some adversity and the need for compassion in our world today. Once you read this book, you will be inspired to create a mindset to win compassionately."

Frank Carbajal

Founder of Silicon Valley Latino Leadership Summit Co-Author Building the Latino Future
Co-Author Latinx Business Success

A JOURNEY TO COMPASSION

Learning to Stand Firm in the Face of Pain

FELIPE MERCADO, Ed.D

A JOURNEY TO COMPASSION

Cover Design by Marco Alvarez

Layout by LDG Juan Manuel Serna Rosales

Printed in the United States of America

ISBN: 978-1-957058-31-3

Library of Congress Control Number: 2022922405

FIG
FACTOR
MEDIA

TABLE OF CONTENTS

INTRODUCTION

Today, you do not have to look far to find a community referred to as the hood, the barrio, the trap, or the block. In these neighborhoods, you also don't have to look far to know someone, or know of someone, who has been shot, killed, locked up, addicted to drugs, or dealing with mental health issues. To make matters worse for those who live in these environments, they often grow immune to the violence and suffering they're exposed to from a very early age. Day in and day out, these individuals walk through trauma-riddled environments, and for some, there may never be an escape. Society does little to help people in these spaces feel safe or to change the harsh reality for this marginalized population.

Humans who identify as being of color, impoverished, and culturally different from the "American standard" often lose hope in society, feeling it wasn't created for someone who "looks like" them. They tend to find other ways to belong in the world. It's no wonder that so many young people growing up in these underprivileged conditions look up to the hustler, the gangster, or the pimp as role models or for protection—because those are the only people they see who look like them and come from the same place. These figures are often seen as having achieved success, even without a strong educational background. The hustler, the pimp, or the athlete are often the only aspirational figures in these environments.

For many children and youth of color living in poverty, these types of role models are the only ones who seem to understand them. They don't often see other positive role models who look like them or understand their reality. The school system and other community structures frequently punish these youth for merely adapting to and surviving their daily circumstances. Many ignore the historical injustices imposed on these populations long before these children were even born. Most people from adverse conditions don't believe we "deserve better" or that "good" opportunities exist for people like us. The school system, communities, and policies need to find more compassionate, humane, culturally rooted, and evidence-based methods of engaging and inspiring children and youth of color, who are born into generational trauma and poverty, instead of punishing, ignoring, or labeling them.

Living in environments surrounded by shootings, domestic violence, drugs, and gangs, it can feel like no one is willing or able to understand how to help people in these conditions. Life feels even harder when you're not accepted, constantly judged for dodging violence every day, and told that you'll never be good enough. Many youth growing up in what I call Poverty 4x (more on this in Chapter 5) must step into adult roles, becoming parents to their younger siblings when their own parents are working, sick, or dealing with drug use or mental health issues. Many of us in Poverty 4x have stayed up late at night, worrying whether our mom or dad would make it home safely—or wondering if they would even come home at all.

As children, many of us felt utterly alone, not knowing what to do or where to go in times of worry. We were constantly at war with the adverse conditions in our homes, with no one there to support or understand us. Furthermore, this diverse population has to deal with oppression and judgment for being born into these conditions, for having darker skin, and for holding traditions or languages that don't fit into the "American standard."

Psychologist Bruce D. Perry describes this ongoing pain as "complex trauma" because, unlike a soldier who returns from war, people living in these adverse conditions can never escape the environments they were born and raised in. This trauma impacts every instance of a person's life. For men of color, in particular, many of us were taught not to show or express our emotions. We were taught to avoid reliving the pain of the past, as society would label us weak if we didn't appear in control or act tough and picture-perfect. Many of us who come from adverse experiences learned to be rigid and passive with our feelings, unconsciously creating an image of what we thought we should be.

As a Latino man in my late thirties, I've become aware of the pain I kept inside for so long, and I now understand where it comes from. I now think of how we can make life more bearable for others experiencing these conditions—or worse.

I have lived with intense pressure—what is called "complex trauma"—since childhood. I couldn't escape it, whether at home, in school, or out in the neighborhood. There were days when I felt pressure from trying to be the child my parents wanted me to be, but never feeling like I was enough. I was constantly being compared to others or told I wasn't good enough. At school, I never felt accepted, often because I didn't meet the state standards due to my language, my culture, and the inherited trauma I already knew was there.

Something inside me always hurt. I learned that it was the shame and constant pain that came from thinking the only way to avoid it was to never let anyone hurt me. From that moment on, I was anxious and afraid that someone would yell at me for not fitting in, or for not meeting their expectations, or blame me for things that had nothing to do with me. Trying my best, doing everything I could, always felt like intense pressure as a kid. But no matter what, it never felt like enough, because nothing I did seemed good enough in the eyes of others—whether it was my parents, teachers, or society at large.

All of these expectations to fit in at home, in school, and in society made me create a force field around my heart. I wouldn't let anyone hurt me anymore. As I locked the pain away and ignored it, I didn't realize how this would affect my health, my life, and my overall well-being. The force field I created trapped my pain, sadness, and worry inside. I learned to cope with this pain by using other outlets. By the age of fourteen, I was homeless, addicted to meth and cocaine, and experiencing suicidal tendencies. I had no idea what I was doing or where I was going. I had little positive support.

When I think back to my junior high or high school years, I don't have many positive memories. I was surrounded by adults who could have helped but chose not to; they judged me instead. I was kicked out of high school multiple times and had to survive homelessness. There was no one at school for me to connect with, no one who cared to listen. Society treated people like me as outcasts, and their actions backed that up. At 14, I never knew what was going to happen next in my life. My thoughts raced constantly. I often wondered if I'd have a place to stay or food to eat. I feared being locked up or shot for being out past curfew or simply trying to find a place to sleep.

My early teens were dangerous and tragic. I did whatever I could to survive with the limited guidance and resources I had. The only people who understood me were the homies on the block. They made me feel safe and taught me how to survive while I was drowning in my pool of pain. We lived in a city that seemed eager to lock us up, and schools that kicked us out.

Most of us came from homes where the primary income was food stamps provided by SNAP (CalFresh in California) and cash aid through Temporary Assistance for Needy Families (TANF). This assistance was critical for my mom, who struggled with mental health issues and a disability that prevented her from working. My dad battled addiction and a lack of education. There were times when our water, electricity, and food were limited or shut off entirely. My grandparents and parents often stood in line at food banks just so we could have a meal. I grew up in a place where many parents were addicted to drugs, had mental health issues, were undocumented, lacked a high school diploma, or had no assets to pass down.

As a child and teenager, I viewed the world as a dog-eat-dog place. I watched my parents and grandparents struggle to provide for themselves and their loved ones. I told myself I would find another way. At that age, I couldn't understand how we lived in a world with people who had yachts and jets, while others—like my family—were struggling to meet basic needs. This mindset filled me with anger and hate during my teenage years because I didn't yet know how to love myself or appreciate the few things going right in my life, something I've learned to see as an adult.

Not understanding how to process my ongoing trauma, I created a character and behaved in ways I thought would keep me alive. I needed to survive my conditions and not appear weak or poor. For almost two decades, I lived feeling worthless, insecure, unprotected, and unloved. Rather than show my pain, I learned to grow cold, to distrust others, and to make money in ruthless ways. From fourteen until about twenty years old, I was homeless and alone. During that time, I masked all my pain by becoming the hustler I thought would help me escape the pain, poverty, broken family, and a community that seemed not to care about people like me.

As I continued down this path, I used money, status, and outward appearances to pretend I was fine, both inside and out. I had no one I could trust, no one who could give me the understanding I needed to open up and be myself, except for my friend, David, and my two brothers. The absence of a positive, understanding parent, family member, or community leader made me feel like I was truly alone in the world.

Learning about neurobiology and neuroscience later in life helped me understand the disconnect I experienced in my brain—the disconnect that prevented me from forming relationships or behaving in socially acceptable ways. The shame I felt and the way society judged me made me constantly feel defensive. I could never truly feel safe. When someone was kind, I always assumed they wanted something from me or wanted me to change who I was.

In recent years, neuroscientists, psychologists, and psychiatrists have revealed how adverse conditions shape human development. As you'll learn in the chapter on Poverty 4x, when someone is raised in these conditions, the architecture of their brain is wired differently. This impacts their mental, physical, spiritual, social, and psychological development.

For decades, society has continued to punish, shame, and belittle vulnerable populations while neglecting to understand their behaviors or the reasons they don't fit into the "status quo." Most professionals and leaders have never been honest about how they've reinforced and perpetuated these adverse experiences for those living in poverty, neighborhoods with high crime, and low-quality schools—or those whose parents struggle with mental health or end up in jail. These failed approaches make youth and children feel like they'll never be able to fit in. When they do conform, they often lose their culture and authenticity, becoming lost. We need new approaches to help these individuals see how sacred, brilliant, and extraordinary their spirit and essence truly are.

When you grow up poor, looked down on for your skin color, and with little hope for the future, it's hard to believe you deserve the good the world has to offer. Many of us who grew up in these conditions have endured, witnessed, and continue to be impacted mentally, physically, and spiritually. This pain sits inside us daily. It's as if we were born into a swimming pool of pain, constantly fighting to reach the surface but drowning under the weight of society's ideals.

Looking back, I wish I had known what I needed then—how to express what I know now and how to advocate for myself. Maybe I wouldn't have struggled for so long. Perhaps I could have given better advice to my youngest brother, Sammy, or my best friend, David. They might still be alive today. Losing two of the most influential people in my life forced me to reflect and eventually led me to this path of compassion. Before then, I was consumed with hate. It wasn't easy to heal after their deaths. I didn't understand how to grieve, and their loss prevented me from moving forward for a long time.

As I wrote this book, I thought deeply about the bond and love that my parents, brothers, and grandparents had lost. I reflected on the disconnection from my culture, my community, and my school. It's critical that we reassess how we support and address issues of trauma, poverty, culture, and mental health in our communities and beyond.

This book offers you the wisdom, game, "consejos," and compassion I wish I could have shared with my brother before he left this earth. Compassion wasn't something I found until after I had children, earned a doctorate, and discovered how to find happiness as an adult. Learning self-compassion, having compassion for others, and letting go of the anger, hate, and resentment that accumulated throughout my life transformed how I see the world, my mental health, and how I choose to spend my time.

I once thought the best career I could have was selling drugs, committing crimes, or ending up in jail. I could never have imagined I would be where I am today. I share this newfound wisdom to help people from similar backgrounds start off with a better beginning, a better present, and a better future.

Each chapter of this book connects to personal experiences—yours or someone else's. Whether you're reading to heal yourself or to help others, begin by setting your mindset in the right place. We're about to take a deep journey into childhood adversity and cultivate compassion in the face of pain. Before we begin, look in the mirror and say these words aloud to yourself. Share them, remember them, and say them whenever you need to. Let these words become a part of you:

You are not a bad person.

You are not a misfit or outcast.

You are not a disappointment.

You are not a broken person.

You are not a failure.

You are not less than anyone

You are good enough as you are.

The world is better because you are in it.

Your experiences will help you carry wisdom.

Your pain will provide you with the power to heal.

Your smile, insight into life, and sense of humor will help bring about change.

Hold on and keep your heart and mind strong.

You will see that what you went through then will make you a better person tomorrow.

The trick is to never let the hate and anger take over and to always remember your authentic self!

You know that person you are proud of.

The one deep down inside that sometimes we have to hide.

Find more ways to be this person and be around others who support this person.

Your story can transform someone's life!

This book also aims to capture the attention of therapists, practitioners, educators, leaders, and policymakers who want to better support individuals who face these conditions throughout their lifetime. In each chapter, you'll find a quote that sets the tone and captures the essence of my life in those moments. These quotes provide insight into my mindset during that time. Poetry and Hip Hop have significantly influenced my life; they helped me through some of my darkest days and gave me perspectives no one else was offering at that time.

In many chapters, after the quotes, you'll find practices or self-reflections to help you or someone going through similar experiences start finding new ways to think about their situation.

Whether you've lived through these events or are helping someone who has, I hope we can find ways to heal the trauma we carry.

The final chapters demonstrate how transformation can happen by working on oneself, and how suffering can create wisdom and social justice if we are open to confronting fear, shame, and hurt. By walking through the pain, we can see what lies on the other side.

These raw and authentic experiences reflect the suffering that children living in poverty and trauma-riddled environments face daily, and how we can better understand and transform these experiences to support better outcomes for this population. This book also illuminates the lessons I've learned and the consequences I've faced from choices, mistakes, and the lack of knowledge and wisdom I carried for much of my life.

As each chapter builds, the reader will come to understand how trauma impacts a child's development, mindset, and sense of worth in this world. You'll also find strategies and insights that can help create different environments and approaches—or help someone realize that surviving each day against all odds makes them a true survivor.

CHAPTER 1:

CHILDHOOD

—————

My first concrete memory of my parents fighting was when I was five years old. I remember hearing my mom yell at my dad, their voices getting louder and louder by the minute. Then came the pushing and slapping—each time escalating until, in a blur, I saw my mom slam through the coffee table in the living room. I froze, unable to do anything. These were the two people who were supposed to show me love, and yet, they were at war with each other.

I remember thinking my mom was going to die. I had never seen so much blood before—streaming down her arms and elbows. But the very next day, there she was, cooking in the kitchen as if nothing had happened. My dad, sitting on the couch rolling a joint, acted like it was just another day—no coffee table, no evidence of the fight. This was the cycle of trauma at home, and I couldn't understand it. I never saw them truly make up. I was sent to my room after their cage-like fights, left to sit alone with my thoughts. And we never talked about what happened.

My dad had been married before and had two daughters, but in 1984, two years before I was born, he married my mom. One day, out of the blue, my mom decided to tell me the "truth" about how I came to be. She said I was conceived because my dad had taken her birth control away—something I didn't understand at the time. From that moment on, I began to wonder if I was even wanted. Did my parents love me? Did they want me in their lives? As a child, I craved their attention but didn't know how to get it.

I knew my mom was different from the other moms. She was sick all the time, often sleeping or resting after the simplest activities. People called her crazy, and other families judged her for not working. I didn't understand what she was going through, but I knew I had to help her in any way I could. My dad, on the other hand, seemed preoccupied with making money—often through side jobs or selling drugs like marijuana, cocaine, or heroin.

As a boy, I just wanted to be happy. I wanted my parents to love me the way I saw other kids' parents love them. But as time passed, I watched my family fall apart. My mom went on permanent disability around the time I started kindergarten, and I made it my mission to make her happy, even if I didn't fully understand her illness.

As sons of wounded fathers, we are conditioned to bury our pain. We're taught that vulnerability is weakness, and to survive, we must hide our emotions and turn a blind eye to the turmoil in our families. We internalize the belief that silence is strength, but in doing so, we distance ourselves from the very healing we need.

Watching my parents fight was a significant part of my childhood. The physical and verbal abuse was relentless, and the way they acted like everything was fine afterward made me feel like their entire relationship was a lie. What they showed me was an unhealthy example of love, one that has stayed with me for years. Many men around me, including myself, grew up in environments where expressing love felt impossible. As a result, we didn't know how to give or receive it.

I learned to fear my dad. He rarely showed any love, and I was too young to protect myself or my mom. When my parents weren't fighting with each other, my dad would take out his anger on me. My mom, too sick or too exhausted most of the time, couldn't intervene.

As my mom got sicker each day, withdrawing more into herself, I felt helpless. She stopped going out, became thinner, and spent most of her time in her room. I desperately wanted to help her, to protect her from my dad, but I didn't know how. I was just a kid, watching her pain and feeling my own. Sometimes, when my mom was having a bad day, she would take her frustration out on me, which strained our relationship even more.

When discipline came, my parents didn't hold back. If their words failed, they turned to physical beatings. It often felt like they only came together as a couple when they were punishing me. I couldn't defend myself—I felt powerless and hopeless. Their methods of punishment scarred me mentally, physically, and spiritually, especially when they both unleashed their anger on me. Even when they were mad at each other, it somehow always felt like it was my fault.

Despite this, my childhood experiences taught me resilience. They gave me the toughness to handle life's challenges. But at the same time, they filled me with anger and insecurity, which I eventually turned outward toward others. Raised in an environment where pain was the currency, it was the only thing I knew how to give and receive.

To my dad, I was never enough. His words cut me to the core, leaving scars that ran deeper than I understood at the time. I can't remember a moment of shared joy or laughter with him. He was the first person to break my heart. The idea of being loved became something I no longer believed in. If my parents couldn't love or accept me, who would?

These thoughts turned my mind dark. I began to believe that I would never be accepted or loved unless I did what others wanted, even if it meant losing myself. My brain wasn't wired to understand healthy relationships, so I pushed away anyone who tried to get close. Fear of rejection rooted in constant criticism and feelings of inadequacy became my norm.

There was so much abuse and neglect in those formative years. I didn't fully understand what my parents were struggling with, but I knew I hated that they couldn't find peace or be the parents I needed. As a child, I often prayed that they would stop being so angry and get the help they so desperately needed. I yearned for the normalcy and happiness that other families seemed to have.

Now, looking back, I understand that they were dealing with their own unhealed trauma—trauma passed down to me in a time where they had no resources, no support, and no understanding of how to heal. Their harsh discipline—with belts, switches, and kneeling on rocks—was likely how they had been disciplined. It reflected generational pain, perhaps even tied to how our ancestors were treated.

By the age of six, I was already running into the streets, searching for the love, connection, and acceptance I couldn't find at home. The pain inside me was growing each day. I learned to fight, lie, and navigate life with a chip on my shoulder. I absorbed the unspoken rule of "what happens here, stays here," terrified that revealing our home life to anyone would result in my parents going to jail, losing what little we had, or me ending up in foster care. That fear silenced me.

I grew up believing that abuse—whether emotional, verbal, or physical—was normal. This left me confused because I wanted to be good, but negativity surrounded me. No matter how hard I tried, I never felt good enough for my parents. They compared me to others—my dad's daughters, my cousins—and it deepened my feelings of inadequacy. I always felt like they were better than me, like I was missing something fundamental.

Over time, those painful words became a voice in my head, shaping my thoughts and actions. Even when I tried to do good, it felt like the world was against me. At school, I wasn't valued for who I was, and at home, I was immersed in a world of drug use, violence, and mental health struggles.

Navigating an environment steeped in criminal behavior taught me how to be good at being bad. I learned to steal to feed myself, to fight to protect myself, and to carry the weight of my anger wherever I went. On the streets, being wrong was often seen as being right. Violence earned you respect and notoriety, things I desperately sought in place of the love I couldn't get at home.

Eventually, my choices caught up with me, and I ended up in jail. It was there that I began to truly reflect on how intergenerational trauma had shaped me. I had a son, and the desire to break the cycle weighed heavily on me, but I didn't yet know how. The pain I carried from childhood was still unresolved, and I knew I had to face it in order to create a better future for him—and for myself.

Don't take anything personally. Nothing others do is because of you. What others say and do is a projection of their own reality. When you are immune to the opinion and actions of others, you won't be the victim of needless suffering."

—Don Miguel Ruiz, The Four Agreements:

A Toltec Wisdom Book

Don Miguel Ruiz, a well-known Mexican author, speaks of the Smokey Mirror. He describes how we often adopt society's version of who we are and what we should be, becoming trapped in a fog of false beliefs. This fog clouds our vision, blocking us from seeing our true selves. Instead, we are consumed by anger, hate, and negativity. According to Toltec wisdom, we are all light—pure love and pure light—but in the fog, we only see darkness. We start to believe the lies that we are inadequate, flawed, or undeserving.

Revisiting childhood pain can seem pointless or even terrifying. Yet, to heal, we must confront the past. We must look back to understand where the pain began and how it held us back from becoming the best versions of ourselves. Healing starts with seeing beyond the lies we've been told about who we are and embracing our true selves. For those who carry this pain, healing begins with learning to forgive and love yourself. Mistakes are part of life, but it's up to us to learn from them. Mistakes become lessons, and when we grow from them, they turn into wisdom.

No one is perfect—not even the greatest minds. Failure is often the best teacher. In this space of reflection, we begin to forgive ourselves and others. Forgiveness is not about excusing the past but allowing it to rest, letting go of the hold it has on us, and setting our soul free.

As we uncover what has held us back, we start to see who we truly are and the difference we can make in our world. It can help to resurface both the good and bad memories from your childhood. Write them down, reflect on them, and ask yourself: What do you feel when you think of the past? How have those feelings shaped who you've been, and how do they shape who you want to become?

When bad memories arise, find forgiveness for yourself first. As children, we didn't always have the capacity to protect ourselves or make the right choices. We needed to hear words of comfort and reassurance, like "It's going to be okay," "I love you," "You are a blessing," "I'm sorry," and "I'm here for you." My parents never told me these things, so I had to rely on the teachings of my grandparents about our ancestors—to live with honor in the short time we have on this earth. Most importantly, don't forget to love yourself. Not only do you deserve love, but so do others.

Allow the good memories to remind you that love can exist even when hate tries to take over. Remember, even our parents were learning how to live and become adults. They made mistakes, often without knowing how to admit them. Understanding this can help wash away the hate and replace it with empathy. This insight will guide you through your trauma, helping you rediscover who you were before the hate, trauma, and ego took over.

CHAPTER 2:

MEXICANO

When I was a little boy, I perceived my life as a curse. Right at birth, when others would be getting to know their parents and getting the much-needed touch, affection, and bonding, I had to live in an incubator for over a month. I was removed from this experience, as I was dealing with heart issues when I arrived, and this machine supported my heart's development. Trauma and neuroscience experts report that this type of start for any baby will cause a human's brain to be wired differently than someone that does not have this experience. The impact of a baby not bonding with their parents and getting that sense of safety and security at birth already cause conditions that will make it difficult for a human to form healthy relationships. This is a way to take a village, so a child and parents always have someone to support, as this sense of connection, belonging, and safety is crucial for the baby and the parents to grow.

Many told me that my parents used drugs before, during, and after the pregnancy, but I don't know. I knew that my dad had taken my mom's birth control away and that I was the consequence. My mother herself spoke this information. Like many others in the United States, I was born into intergenerational poverty and trauma. Dealing with poverty, lack of education, racism, and other barriers made it hard for my parents to be there for themselves or me. They were not educated, they struggled to find excellent and constant work, and they were dealing with a legacy of addiction and oppression, which did not afford them or their ancestors a peaceful way of life to live in this country. Both my mom and dad were first-generation Mexican-Americans struggling to do their best while figuring out how to be parents.

At an early age, it was clear to me that I had to find love in other places. I could not escape my parents' anger and pain. Holding onto this trauma, they took it out on one another. My grandparents' care for me was my only escape from the toxicity and turbulence at home with my parents. From the ages of two to about five, my grandparents were responsible for any values and lessons instilled in me to this day. Being in my grandparents' homes gave me the best memories of my childhood. Unfortunately, my grandparent's home was not my permanent residence, and I would only stay with them during the week when my mom was working, and my dad was committed to "side jobs."

When my parents weren't around, I was usually with my mom's parents, Nina and Pascual Juarez. They would take care of me for a large part of the week. They did everything they could to teach me to be respectful and to prepare me for the real world. The first lesson my abuelo taught me was, "necesitas ir a la escuela para seguir adelante." He would say, "Look at my hands; I have no medical benefits, I have to work every day with no days off in the hot sun or the cold, and I make the very minimum a person can make here in the United States. You need to go to school and get ahead!" He would say to me, "Necesitas seguir adelante, and you will not have to suffer like this; this is what I want for you."

At my dad's parents' house, Hermelindo and Maria Mercado, I was spoiled with all sorts of homegrown fruits and vegetables. My dad's father was well known for selling this mixture of liquid and a cannabis plant for arthritis. My Grandma Maria's house was tiny, but her garden seemed more extensive than her whole house. Her backyard had this small patio area where my uncles would barbeque. There was another grassy area with the clothesline running across the lawn where she would hang and dry her laundry.

My Grandma Maria had her garden full of lemon trees, avocado trees, squash, you name it. She was the vegetable queen and an herbal goddess in my eyes. In her front yard, she had this huge tree surrounded by gardens with the most beautiful flowers. Grandma Maria's house was one of my favorite places to visit when I was a kid. I remember when she would ask me to water her fruits and vegetables. For her to ask me to help her in her garden or to ask me to water the grass was an honor. In this environment, I had friends who lived in the neighborhood, which made going to her house more fun. I could play there all summer. My Grandma Maria was a loving soul to everyone she was around. She always had lemongrass tea, arroz con leche, or canela (cinnamon tea).

Grandma Maria endured much suffering from being displaced from her family as a teenager. I was told she was a young girl with years of her life taken from her. The story goes that when she was fifteen, she was gathering tea leaves and was kidnapped. The man who had abducted her happens to be my grandfather, Hermelindo Mercado. It is said that he tied her up to his horse and rode off with her, escaping her small village in Mexico. She would eventually arrive in Texas, travel to Nebraska, and finally make a new home in Sanger, California.

I believe my Grandma Maria lost her identity and never had the chance to see her family or where she came from ever again. She had to learn to conform to this new life at a very young age and would give birth to seven children, only boys. My dad was the baby of his family, and it is said that he was spoiled by his mom but treated cruelly by his father. My Grandma Maria's life consisted of raising the children, working, cooking, cleaning, washing, and finding ways to stay connected to her roots. She grew her herb gardens and brought what she remembered as a curandero, a healer of her family. Growing up, we didn't have iPhones or apps to keep us from learning about what was in front of us. Observing my Grandma Maria while I was a little boy helped me understand that in life, love, music, and food made us bond and could make anything better. The pain, suffering, and loss that I can only imagine her going through when she was fifteen motivated me every day and every bit of my soul. I would be determined to find ways to live my life as Grandma Maria did.

I don't know much about my dad's father, Hermanlindo Mercado. My memories of him are primarily snapshots in my head. I remember seeing him ride his bike to the store and sometimes taking me to get a lollipop or other candy.

I don't know if they had a car, my dad's parents. And oddly enough, I do have a vague memory of him tying my hands to the kitchen table as punishment for something I must have done. I can't say exactly what I was punished for, but I remember that incident. He died when I was in preschool. I remember my dad coming to pick me up from preschool that day. I knew something was up with him because I had never seen such a sad look on his face. When his dad died, it was the first time I saw my dad cry. It was the first time I saw him physically and emotionally hurt. I could see that my dad wished he had a better relationship with his father. My dad seemed to be bothered by the fact that I had spent so much time and formed a relationship with his father. Something they never figured out how to do. Sometimes it seemed like my dad hated me because of the way his father showed his love for me as his grandson.

When you are from a family and live in conditions where talking about others is seen as gossip, especially when speaking of men and placing them in a bad light, it's considered a horrible thing, sort of dishonorable to the man being talked about. For men of color, it is shameful and too emotional to relive the past or to speak of your mistakes. Because of that mindset, many things are unsaid and are left in the shadows. These shadows are dark spaces that often remain untouched and can leave a person feeling dead inside, and are why we search to fit in with outside society. We are not healed nor love ourselves enough to tend to our hurt. Let's be real, sometimes we don't know where to start, who the right person to ask that won't judge us, and the words to even begin to use. On top of this, if anyone knew we were thinking about being vulnerable, we would be ridiculed, hit, and shamed. This makes it hard for us to be brave enough to tell our real story!

My mom used to work at a clinic before she went on disability. So, I was babysat by either of my grandparents when she had to go to work. When I would get dropped off at Grandma Maria's house, I would sometimes see her get down and angry. I would look at her and watch her as she would visit her neighbors and talk mostly to vent about her frustrations, her comrades as she would call them. Most of my cousins would sometimes be there, too; and they were all pretty cool to me. But there was one cousin whose behavior I didn't get.

I couldn't understand how he liked to touch himself. That made me uncomfortable whenever he was around. I was used to watching my parents fighting and throwing each other around, but his behavior made being around him creepy. I thought he was weird. He tried to be around my other cousins, but they didn't like him either. Somehow, we all knew he was not the kind of person to get close to or to be alone with. When we didn't hang out with him, he would try his best to crack an inappropriate or derogatory joke about his behavior. I never understood that guy and thought the only bad thing about staying at Grandma Maria's at times was when he came over. Some way or another, my gut told me whatever he was doing and experiencing had to be strange, and it wasn't right for me to be around. I always stayed far away from him. This bothered me because I never knew how to make sense of his behavior until I got older. I would learn why it is people do the things they do.

Each of my grandparents shared stories with me and made me feel happy when I was a boy. I was so proud to be their grandchild! But as I matured, I lost who I was to society's ideals, rather than staying true to who I wanted to be. During the peak of my happiness as a child, I remember I would walk into my grandparents' home and kiss both my grandparents; they would give me pan dulce in return. It was the best feeling. Then they showed me how to water their garden and let me freely explore all around their house. I used to enjoy these rare moments with them while my parents drank coffee, and they all sat around and talked.

Both of my grandmas made homemade flour tortillas. Living in a Mexican household, this is one of the most special treats you can have, homemade tortillas. My Grandma Maria, almost every morning, would make lemongrass tea, arroz con leche that we usually ate with our pan dulce. I remember the smell of tea; it would make my soul jump and my heart feel full. When I was younger, I didn't feel we were poor. My grandparents did a great job of having traditions, love, food, and good music to make life feel worth living. As I went into school, life was changing, and I became ungrateful for the richness of our traditions because these were not aspects that school considered at the time that made a person like me feel accepted or intelligent or essential.

Watching my grandparents work in the fields amazed me with their work ethic. How fast they worked with the limited resources that they had. It was hot in the summer and cold in the winter, but they never took a vacation or had health benefits from working every day. When I was about four and five years old, I would help them. Seeing how hard manual labor can be and watching my grandparents work the fields was a constant reminder that I needed to be educated and keep pushing forward in life. I would go with them to the store to cash their paychecks and see how they were treated compared to other groups of people in town. Store clerks and cashiers would be so biased toward them. People would only speak to them in English. Since my grandparents only knew Spanish, people would get frustrated with them for not speaking proper English and would shame or make fun of them for having such a broad Mexican accent. They never attended school here, so they did not communicate with American English standards.

My parents would share stories with me of my grandparents' struggles back in their home country of Mexico and the hardships they experienced. I could only imagine how that impacted their upbringing. I would hear stories of how they had to eat out of a trash can, wear the same clothes every day, or labor in the fields for very little pay. During my whole life, I had listened to all the ways my grandparents had to live to survive when they were children and teens. I believe this is why they were strict with me, were overly protective, and probably why disciplined me in ways that they thought were trying to protect me from the bigger world.

My Abuelo Pascual, my mom's dad, taught me to be proud of who I was. He would tell me that education was the only way out of poverty. He would say that I could be treated like a first-class citizen with it. My abuelo was a curandero, a healer, and a medicine man—he used natural herbs to cure pain for others in his village and when he moved to California. I loved him entirely with his deep spirit and warrior's heart. My Abuela Nina was strict, but she provided us with unconditional love and guidance that I can say our youth are missing nowadays. Some of us nowadays can be entitled and act in a way that doesn't respect ancestry or aging. As my Abuelo Pascual aged, it would piss me off to hear people say he was going crazy. I wasn't able to comprehend what people were saying about him. I started hearing conversations like this because, apparently, my grandfather had supposedly shot somebody. It was said this apparent incident had happened one day after he experienced a mental breakdown. My abuelo spent some time in jail but was released due to a medical condition.

My abuelos have strong cultural roots that have helped me appreciate my roots. From our homemade tortillas to the stories and the language, my grandparents did all they could to teach me, to guide me, and to help me understand that my culture and language are strengths that I carry within me. The only thing I did not learn was how to talk about what was happening at home because I was constantly hit with some bible verse or expected to act perfect around my mom and dad. I didn't feel my grandparents would believe me if I told them how horrible my parents were to me. My parents always succeeded in making themselves look good in front of their parents and made it seem like I was the little devil. These experiences forced me to see the world through the lens of poverty, oppression, Mexican culture, the Catholic religion, crime, and domestic violence. I never shared or expressed these feelings. It was all in the force field.

Ever since I could think on my own, I always felt like I wanted to help people like my abuelos and my abuelas or people like my parents, people who I saw suffer from the worse kind of oppression, poverty, and hardship that seemed to erode their liberation and sense of value in this world. My people, my Mexican-born abuelos, were often oppressed by the "system," but they remain the same people who showed me love, culture, and beauty. Most of my interactions stem from living in my community with brown people who were mostly field workers on government assistance, sometimes undocumented, used or sold drugs, had been in and out of jail, and encompassed no form of a solid education. Some of us were written off by the more significant part of society. We were shamed into thinking that our language and culture were not good enough. But just like my grandparents told me, life will be hard for you, and life will get more complex, and it will be tough for people like us, but we have to find a way to "seguir adelante."

I grew up as a young Mexican boy in a town where you were shamed for only speaking Spanish and being proud of your own culture. Being poor, in addition to being Mexican, made it hard growing up because I always felt judged by others. My family was on food stamps, how they dressed, the cars they drove, where they worked, where we lived, and even how we would pronounce words was viewed as too different. As a family, it seemed like everywhere we went, we were not only judged, but others looked at us as if we were weird or not as worthy as other people around town. Being a Mexican kid, I grew up believing that the world hated me, my family, and my culture. The place I grew up made me feel as though I didn't belong there. With no sense of belonging, I needed to fight every day to be seen and heard.

Almost everywhere I searched outside of my grandparent's home, I saw that our traditions were being ridiculed, and I was quickly learning to be ashamed of where I came from and who I was. In school, I was taught that they were different because my grandparents and ancestors came from another country, spoke a different language, and had different practices. My grandparents picked grapes and did other seasonal agricultural work for a living. They would put on their gear and take their Thermos® and tacos daily during the season. I remember they would come back so tired from the fields and tell me they had barely made any money. I always wanted my grandparents to have more than they deserved because they worked so hard.

Sometimes, I would help them pick grapes when they babysat me when I was young. It was fun at first until it would get too hot or too cold, especially if you got whacked by the vines; it would hurt like hell. My grandparents and the traditions they shared with us when it came to making tamales, and tortillas, holding annual family Christmas lunches, and just giving them a kiss when we saw them was something that I always looked forward to as a child. The hard part is that my parents were struggling with drug addiction, mental health issues, and getting along with each other, which led to them fighting for many days of my life. Or it was me being punished in some way, shape, or form. During my entire childhood, my mom dealt with mental health and other disabilities, and my dad never talked about his feelings and seemed to take his anger out on us in many different ways or by escaping from his reality by using drugs.

"I am Joaquin, lost in a world of confusion, caught up in the whirl of a gringo society, confused by the rules, scorned by attitudes, suppressed by manipulation, and destroyed by modern society."

—Rodolfo "Corky" Gonzales, "I am Joaquin/Yo soy Joaquin"

———————

Many people from these backgrounds are not prepared for the conditions they will face to be who they are in society. It starts young. The system and sometimes "others" do all they can to make us hate our culture, language, where we come from, and, in turn, each other. Once the backlash kicks in from others who hold on to a more colonial view of how things should be in our world, some of us tend to do all we can to fit in to survive. When this happens, we become detached and begin to speak like them, act like them, and before we know it, we are just like them. Those also are called the naysayers. When we do not teach our children to celebrate the culture they are born into, the language and traditions associated with their people, many of us do not understand our roots and why it has been so challenging for us to make it here. Although things can be challenging being a person of color in today's world, it is essential for you to be proud of who you are, to be proud of where you came from, to hold the honor for your family and its roots, and know that this is what makes you unique, sacred and connected to who you indeed are.

Not being accepted at home or school made me question my purpose in this world, and soon I grew to hate my life, school, and even my own culture. As a person, I grew insecure, which caused me always to want to prove something because I never felt good enough. Being treated like I always had to prove myself impacted my attitude, behavior, and how I saw the world. It made me mad at my parents, who I had felt could have been there to offer me unconditional support or a person who would judge me, shame me, and make me feel unwanted. This chip on my shoulder caused me to walk around life ready to let loose at any time to prove who I was at a very young age. Carrying this trauma and not having people to show me what unconditional love was for myself and others made it easy to push anyone away who tried to get close or tap into my heart or soul.

Only when you love where you came from and understand everything that makes you the person you truly are, even before you were born, will you begin to have the wisdom and strength to be who you are in this world. I intend that you learn to become aware and observe what it is that does an excellent job of trying to deny your existence. Always remember that you came so far on your journey; did you believe you would get this far? I want you to remember who you are and where you came from because, being in the darkness, you alone can transpire that light within yourself to make a change, which is a powerful thing. Remember that and always keep that light, bright inside of you. We often worry about the mountains ahead, but we forget that the mountains we have already climbed were just as challenging. You naturally have this resilience, making you who you are today. You must dig deep so that you do not lead with this trauma that has become a typical pattern of who we are if we have not got the help or support we need, but with the wisdom, you carry from your ancestors and others who came before you.

CHAPTER 3:

KINDERGARTEN

Growing up in poverty as a Mexican, I always felt forced to adapt to be like everyone else, especially once I started school. I felt that I had to talk, behave, and learn a certain way, and if I didn't, I would be punished by my teachers and judged by the other students. I never imagined that being Mexican would cause me trauma throughout my life, because before school, I was a happy kid. I loved tending to my Grandma Maria's garden or helping my Abuelo Pascual around the house. Life felt like an everyday adventure. That was my happy place — the way I wanted to live. But when I started school, I quickly noticed how my teachers looked at me, how they treated me differently from the other students. I always felt it was because I dressed differently, spoke fluent Spanish, and didn't engage much in the Americanized activities in class.

Navigating the school system became a new challenge, learning how to survive while still trying to love who I was and where I came from. I quickly learned that by my teachers' standards, I wasn't "smart enough," and on top of that, I was singled out because of my language. Spanish was my first language, but in school, it was treated as a barrier rather than a gift. The poverty my parents couldn't overcome created an environment of unhappiness at home, making it difficult for me to develop an optimistic or compassionate mindset. Yet, despite the chaos at home, I remained grateful for the Spanish my grandparents taught me and the culture they instilled in me. It's painful to admit that, today, English is my first language. The school system shamed the Spanish and Mexican culture out of me. And just like many other children, I abandoned my language and culture in an attempt to fit in.

As an adult, I now recognize the parallels between my own experience and that of my ancestors, who were forced to forget their language and traditions. The same system that erased their culture was now erasing mine. Children should never be ashamed of their language or their culture. Don't ever lose who you are just to fit in. Being proud of your roots is essential to finding happiness.

As a child, I wasn't taught to love myself in school. My teachers didn't encourage me to honor my culture or embrace my language. Instead, I was made to feel stupid for not knowing English well enough, even though I felt capable and smart inside. My struggles began when I had to assimilate into the norms of American society. I was forced to behave the way teachers expected me to, which meant I couldn't be my true self. I could no longer pee behind a tree, shower with a hose in my batman underwear, or speak proudly in Spanish. It was all deemed too savage. On top of that, I began to realize that my parents were considered poor, a label I had never understood until school showed me how different I was from the other kids.

School wasn't just about teaching me English or how to follow rules—it was about erasing my identity, teaching me that my family, with its rich culture and values, wasn't good enough. I was learning that, to be accepted, we had to fit the colonial mold: to have college degrees, stable jobs, and celebrate every American holiday as if that was the only valid expression of life. Anything less was deemed unworthy. But even as a child, I felt the violent undercurrent of this forced assimilation.

This wasn't education; it was colonization in action—a systematic stripping away of my heritage, language, and sense of self. Every lesson in class subtly told me that the world my ancestors built, the language they spoke, and the traditions they cherished had no place in this "modern" world. I was meant to believe that to be "American," I had to reject everything that made me *me* . I was to see my Mexican roots as inferior, my culture as something to shed, and my identity as something to abandon in the pursuit of whiteness.

I resented it deeply. Even as a child, I knew I didn't want to fit into this colonial mold—a mold that erased my spirit, my voice, my history. What they called "education" was actually an erasure of my family's legacy, a suffocation of my soul, and a blatant attempt to make me conform to a system that was never designed for us. It wasn't just about learning the language of the oppressor; it was about surrendering everything sacred that we carried with us.

But we don't have to fit into that mold. We don't have to accept the lie that our ancestors' knowledge and way of life were lesser. Reclaiming who we are—our language, our culture, our roots—is an act of resistance. We have to dismantle this internalized colonization and remember that our existence, in itself, is a form of rebellion. Our traditions, our skin, our language—everything they tried to make us hate—are our strength, not our weakness.

I refused to let their expectations define me. And today, I refuse to be part of a legacy that devalues where I come from. Reclaiming our identity is the most powerful act of decolonization we can engage in. We must return to the wisdom of our ancestors, to the strength of our people, and to the beauty of everything we've been taught to suppress. We are not here to fit into the colonial narrative—we are here to break it.

By the time I entered kindergarten, I was already being held back. They wouldn't let me start school because I didn't know enough English. I was put into a pre-kindergarten program to learn my letters and numbers in English. It was confusing for me, as I wasn't used to speaking English at home, and some of the sounds and words felt foreign on my tongue.

I began to internalize that shame. My name, Felipe, and my fluent Spanish were no longer sources of pride—they became sources of embarrassment. The more I assimilated, the more I felt like an imposter. I tried to fit in, but no matter how hard I worked, it never seemed enough. Even when I asked for help, my teachers accused me of cheating, and soon the other students were told not to help me either. I started to believe that I would never be good enough—never smart enough, never American enough.

The frustration and pain I felt began to manifest as anger. I remember one day in kindergarten, during a soccer game, a couple of boys started arguing with me. One of them pushed me, and without thinking, I started swinging at him and his friend. Within seconds, I had them both up against the fence. I didn't know how else to respond because fighting was what I had seen growing up. If you were disrespected, you fought back. That's what my parents did, and I thought that's what I was supposed to do, too.

After that, I was labeled as the "little Mexican kid who fights." It was hard to show my intelligence or how good I felt deep down inside when I was already seen as a troublemaker. The trauma I carried from home compounded with the challenges I faced in school, leaving me feeling like I was constantly falling short. The only moments of joy came when I walked to school with my friends or spent time in the neighborhood.

One morning, my friend Cheeto and I stumbled upon a payphone that seemed to be raining coins. We couldn't believe it. As two poor kids, finding all that money felt like hitting the jackpot. We started collecting the coins, thinking we were rich, only to get in trouble at school for "stealing." We didn't even realize what we had done, but the teachers and principal didn't care about our intentions. We were just two Mexican kids, caught in a situation beyond our understanding, and we were punished for it. That day, I learned that no matter what I did or didn't do, my story wouldn't be heard. I would always be judged by how I looked and where I came from.

That experience left a lasting scar. It was just one of many moments that made me feel ashamed of being Mexican. From that point forward, I didn't want to speak Spanish anymore. I was searching for a new identity, one that would allow me to fit into a world that didn't seem to have a place for me.

"When I was five years old, my mother always told me that happiness was the key to life. When I went to school, they asked me what I wanted to be when I grew up. I wrote down 'happy.' They told me I didn't understand the assignment, and I told them they didn't understand life."

—John Lennon

Back then, we didn't have social media platforms, just the radio and TV. And whenever I saw someone who looked like me on TV, they were almost always portrayed as gangsters—men who dressed and acted like cholos. It was like society wanted me to believe that this was the only path for someone like me. My dad, my uncles, my cousins—they all had that style, but their lives weren't glamorous or something to admire.

As I struggled to be a good student and earn praise from my teachers, the fights at home intensified. But the approval I got from my friends for doing the wrong things outweighed any positive feedback I could get from school. No matter how much I wanted to fit in at school, I found myself compromising my integrity and honor just to survive.

I prayed every night to be good, to be as smart as everyone else. But the more I tried, the more I felt like an outsider. My parents and teachers didn't see the real me—they saw the travieso, the troublemaker. And with that label hanging over me, I began to question who I was and whether I would ever be good enough.

Reflection/Practice:

Take a moment to reflect on your own experiences of identity and belonging. Have you ever felt pressured to change who you are to fit into someone else's expectations? Write down those moments and the emotions tied to them. Ask yourself: What parts of yourself did you lose in the process? How can you reclaim those parts of your identity that were taken from you?

Practice self-compassion as you explore these feelings. Remember, healing begins when we embrace who we are, where we come from, and reject the narratives that seek to diminish our worth. You don't need permission to be your authentic self. You've always been enough.

CHAPTER 4:

TRAVIESO

By the age of eight, I had already been labeled a *travieso* — the troublemaker. My parents reinforced this image so deeply that one year, for my birthday, they bought me a cake with an airbrushed devil holding a red pitchfork. The devilish grin, the pointy black eyebrows—it was their way of celebrating the little devil they believed I was becoming. I have a picture of that cake, with its mischievous face, capturing the perception my parents had of me. They laughed as they brought it out, proud of their choice, not realizing how this image was shaping my identity and how I saw myself.

I didn't realize then how much this thinking would shape my childhood, but looking back, it damaged me in ways I didn't fully understand. I learned to suppress my emotions, to wear the mask of the troublemaker, to cope by being the tough kid others feared or admired. I started to fit the role they assigned to me, not because I wanted to, but because it was easier to hide behind it than confront the growing pain inside.

As I started becoming more independent, my dad didn't like it. He was jealous of my friendships, angry when I found joy or safety in others. He wasn't the type to have fun or even use the word. Whenever I wanted to play or go outside, he'd make me stay inside and clean the apartment. It was his way of controlling me, of keeping me from becoming who I wanted to be. I had little autonomy, so I spent a lot of time alone with my thoughts, dreaming of a life where I could finally be happy.

I remember imagining a place where everyone was loved unconditionally, where people were accepted and supported no matter where they were in life. As the negative thoughts built up over time, I started to fantasize about darker things—ways to hurt myself, confront my father, or escape my reality altogether. My only refuge was my *Abuela Nina's* house, but even that was taken away as my parents distanced themselves from family while sinking deeper into drug addiction. In their eyes, spending time with my grandparents or any family meant less time making money from drugs.

I didn't understand it then; it was just how life was. But I started to hate myself, and I fell into a deep depression. I became lonely, disconnected, and convinced I didn't belong— at home, at school, or in society. Violence and drug use were constant in my world, making me feel more insecure with each passing day. At school, I was misunderstood, punished, and labeled, but no one ever took the time to ask if I had the tools to change. I felt like a loser, rejected, and broken, and the thought that I was unwanted consumed me. That's when I began to question why I was born and even considered ending my life.

The negativity spiraled. My mind was filled with thoughts like, *I'll never be good enough, I don't deserve love, I'll never find a positive connection with anyone in this world.* I wanted to be a good student and do the right thing, but I didn't know how. As a Hispanic student in a Eurocentric education system, I was forced to conform to standards that didn't value my strengths, knowledge, or talents. My parents couldn't give me the love I needed to thrive, let alone nurture themselves, and that made school an impossible place for me to engage with.

We lived where we could, not where we wanted. We were a poor Mexican family, surviving on food stamps and government aid. My dad worked odd jobs for others, and I was his helper. Money was always scarce, which only worsened the tension at home. My grandparents worked the fields, spoke only Spanish, and sacrificed everything for their family. Yet my parents chose drugs over sacrifice, a decision that still haunts me.

"Feeling like we're about to be in trouble is one of the most common experiences for trauma survivors that we HATE talking about, because it feels like the kinda thing a kid would be worried about. That's because it

WAS—and we're STILL carrying that kind in our head and heart."

—Dr. Glenn Patrick Doyle (Twitter post on August 24, 2022)

————————

For those of us who grow up in poverty or traumatic environments, fitting into the dominant American standard is almost impossible. We are constantly told, in subtle and overt ways, that we don't belong. For people like us, it's crucial to honor our uniqueness, the heritage passed down by our ancestors, without feeling like we'll be punished for doing so. Unfortunately, many of us lose that essence of who we are. We trade it in to be accepted in a world that doesn't value our true selves. In that trade, we lose compassion for ourselves and for others.

But if we choose to embrace who we are and where we come from, we reclaim that essence. We don't need society's validation; we need only to honor ourselves. In a world that tries to beat us down, we must be intentional about creating positive spaces for ourselves. We must live in a way that honors the sacrifices our ancestors made so that future generations can grow with love, compassion, and peace. No matter what has happened to us, we must learn to love every part of who we are.

Often, we don't know how to express our pain with words. Instead, we act out. The more I acted out, the more I was punished—by my parents, by school, by society. Rather than being met with compassion, I was met with judgment, resistance, and arrogance. A child who is scorned, afraid, and labeled as a troublemaker will never find compassion unless someone shows them unconditional love. The wounds I carried as a child, both mentally and physically, fed my negative self-talk. And with every act of discipline or judgment, those wounds deepened.

No one taught me how to regulate my emotions; I only saw people react. This constant negativity left me feeling disengaged, as though I didn't belong. No one in school took the time to know me; they only shamed and disciplined me, assuming I would always get in trouble. They didn't know my journey, my circumstances. But in the streets, just like in school, getting into trouble gave me a certain status. Being tough, being a fighter—that became my identity, because it was how I survived.

When you grow up in poverty and trauma, you're forced to fight hard to own your story. Everyone tries to tell you who you are or how to be. Society will make you feel worthless, evil, and unworthy, but you must remember to hold on to your essence. You lose your power when you start to believe their lies. We are all products of our environment, but if our environment changes, if we find more positive spaces, we can change, too. Deep down, we all want to make good choices. Some of us just need to be taught how, while others still need to believe they can.

Reflection/Practice:

Take a moment to reflect on the labels that have been placed on you throughout your life. Were they given to you by family, society, or perhaps by yourself? How have these labels shaped the way you see yourself, the way you act, and the way you relate to others?

Now, ask yourself: Are these labels a true reflection of who you are? Or are they constructs imposed on you by those who didn't fully understand your journey, your essence?

Write down the labels you've carried and consider which ones you want to let go of. Then, take a step toward reclaiming your true identity—whether it's through self-expression, forgiveness, or simply acknowledging your worth. Remember, your essence is not defined by others' expectations. You have the power to reshape your story. It starts with embracing who you've always been at your core.

CHAPTER 5:

POVERTY 4X

Poverty 4x describes the experience of individuals from minority groups, especially people of color, who endure long-term poverty. This isn't just poverty in the financial sense but a compounded state of being. Poverty 4x means being born into neighborhoods riddled with crime, violence, and systemic issues, while parents struggle with drug addiction, mental health issues, language barriers, lack of education, exploitation, or disabilities. Living in Poverty 4x is like starting life four laps behind everyone else. No matter how fast you try to run, you're constantly playing catch-up, weighed down by generational burdens and a lack of support.

For those who haven't lived this way, it's hard to grasp the gravity of it. These conditions strip parents of the capacity to fully love and nurture their children. They are often drowning in their own unresolved traumas, making it impossible for them to break the cycle of poverty that traps them and their families. As a result, this suffering is passed down, generation after generation, like an unshakable curse.

Children growing up in this environment, without authentic love or positive reinforcement, internalize negative beliefs about themselves and the world. Society labels them as unfit, unwanted, and without value. Instead of living in compassionate, supportive communities, people in Poverty 4x are forced to conform to standards that were never meant for them. They feel unsafe, like outcasts, isolated for not fitting into the "acceptable" mold. This isolation often leads to mental health struggles and addiction—because when you're constantly told you're not enough, numbing the pain feels like the only option. You want to be someone, but the world forces you to be someone else, or worse, tells you you're nothing.

By the time I was six, I knew we were poor. We used food stamps, and I didn't have many clothes. One day in second grade, during a football game at recess, my shirt ripped as I ran for a touchdown. When I got to the office, I couldn't stop crying. I knew my parents wouldn't understand. They wouldn't see the joy of the game; they would only see the torn shirt and what it had cost them.

Luckily, the principal, Mr. Juan Silva, gave me a new Lincoln Elementary T-shirt. It was my first piece of school spirit wear, and I clutched it like a lifeline. He probably thought I was crying out of embarrassment, not realizing I was crying out of fear—fear of what awaited me at home.

That same year, another student and I ranked the highest on the state test in our class. It was the first time I felt proud, the first time I had ever been honored for anything. We were rewarded with breakfast and a shiny pin. But as soon as I saw how people looked at my dad, dressed in his favorite sweats with his shirt tucked into his pants, my pride evaporated. He didn't look like the other well-dressed parents, and the shame of our poverty crept over me like a shadow.

By second grade, I was good at math and starting to grasp English, but my first language, Spanish, was slipping away. We used to speak it when we visited my grandparents, but those visits became less frequent as the distance between us and them grew. The less we saw my grandparents, the more I noticed my parents' struggles. We lived in an alley between O and P streets, and every day as I walked to and from school, I was ashamed of where we lived. I didn't want my friends to know that our front door opened into an alley.

Around this time, my dad's "partner" began taking trips to Mexico, bringing back what they called "product." My dad told me it was rare, that it would make them money, but I soon realized it was drugs. Whenever I got something from the fridge, I had to move bricks of "product" to get to the milk. I didn't fully understand it back then, but I knew it was dangerous. As my dad's addiction worsened, so did our poverty. Eventually, his choices caught up to him, and he ended up in jail.

Seeing my dad in jail was the first time I realized adults didn't have it all figured out. For the first time, I saw him as human— as someone who needed help, just like me. My parents weren't the ideal, loving figures I wished for, but they were struggling too. This didn't excuse the trauma, the violence, or the abuse I experienced, but it gave me a glimpse into why things were the way they were.

In my neighborhood, everyone knew someone who had been to jail. Collect calls from California State Prison became normal in our house. My uncle Ray would call, and I remember singing the ABCs over the phone, thinking how special it was that he called me from his "vacation." But when he came home, he was never the same. Solitary confinement had taken something from him. I learned that jail wasn't just a punishment—it was another prison layered over the one we were already living in.

After my dad got out of jail, we had nowhere to go, so we moved into my grandma Maria's garage. It was tough, and eventually, my parents couldn't take it anymore. We ended up at the Townhouse Motel, where the parking lot became my playground. It was there, throwing a baseball against the walls and playing catch with myself, that I found my only escape from the trauma that replayed daily inside our cramped motel room.

The parking lot of the Townhouse Motel became my sanctuary. I used to look around and wish I had a family like the ones I saw on TV—a family that loved each other, sat down for meals, and didn't solve problems with violence. But my reality was far from that. My family's unresolved anger, violence, and addiction consumed us. I became their punching bag, physically and emotionally.

Growing up in Poverty 4x, I thought this life of struggle, scarcity, and shame was normal. It took me years to realize it wasn't. I share my story because it's important for people like me to understand that we have the power to rewrite our narratives. Escaping the cycle of poverty isn't easy. You can't outrun the pain, and you can't forget how your past shaped you. But healing is possible, and it starts with understanding where you come from.

For those living in Poverty 4x, learning to love yourself is the first step toward breaking the cycle. You have to arm yourself with compassion and refuse to let bitterness or anger control you. This mindset can change everything—whether in the classroom, at home, or in the face of systemic racism. Learning to breathe through the pain, to respond rather than react, is the medicine that protects you from being consumed by the flames of your circumstances.

Growing up as a child, I wanted a family like the ones I used to watch on TV. I wanted a caring family like Will Smith in Fresh

Prince or even being accepted by the Winslows, like Steve Urkel on Family Matters. Families cared for one another, worked out their problems, had a nice home with food, and did not use drugs or physical abuse to cope with their problems. Instead, my family had horrific arguments, my parents beat each other, and I lived with the vilest abuse, feeling neglected from unresolved issues and anger. I became their kid-punching bag, and many of my basic needs were ignored. I remember hating my mom as a kid for not having the ability to wise up or find the strength to leave my dad. Why my dad was so mean and rude to me and my mother was beyond my comprehension. Yet, I knew that I did not want to live this way, and it caused me not to want to live in that house.

"Compassion is an action word with no boundaries. It is never wasted."

—Prince

———————

Most people who have lived in Poverty 4x have been against the odds since the day they were born. Many have been conditioned to believe that poverty, struggle, and feeling "less than" is the normal way of life. That's why I chose to share my story—it's crucial for people living in Poverty 4x to understand how to rewrite their narrative. The only way to escape this reality is to go through it. There is no way to outrun the painful thoughts or the scars of the past.

The hard truth for those living in Poverty 4x is that, if left unhealed, this reality can last a lifetime and beyond, passing from one generation to the next. While we can't control the biases, othering, or racism we face, and we can't single-handedly dismantle poverty or undo the deep wounds of intergenerational trauma, we *can* control how we rise from it. Knowing where you come from, honoring your roots, and embracing your cultural resilience are essential steps toward understanding how you and others view the world. It's in this understanding that real change begins—both for ourselves and for the communities that raised us.

For people living in Poverty 4x, loving yourself is essential. You must learn how not to fan the flames or let them burn you. Not fanning the flames means learning how to breathe, how to respond rather than react in the face of challenges. It means finding peace and centering yourself so that you don't let that angry energy drive you toward self-destruction, self-hate, or broken relationships.

This mindset—of arming yourself with love—can be used in every area of life, from the classroom to the streets, in the face of racism, and in the daily grind of life. Escaping the mental prison that poverty creates is the greatest challenge for people living in these conditions. You feel judged, unsafe, constantly trying to prove yourself. This is the Poverty 4x mindset. But it doesn't have to define you.

Reflection/Practice:

Take a moment to reflect on your own experiences with struggle, whether personal or passed down through generations. How has poverty—or the feeling of being "less than"—shaped how you see yourself and the world? If you've ever felt four laps behind in life's race, consider what that has done to your sense of self-worth and potential.

Write down the emotions and thoughts that come up as you think about these experiences. What narratives have you internalized about your identity, your place in society, and your future? What parts of your story have been written by others, and which parts can you reclaim?

Now, practice compassion for yourself. Remember that no matter the struggles, the key to escaping the mental and emotional prisons built by poverty is to learn how to breathe through the pain and rise above it. Compassion is a tool, a mindset that can transform your reactions into responses, your suffering into strength. In every breath, remind yourself that you are more than your circumstances. You are more than the cards you've been dealt. And in that truth lies your power to rewrite the rest of your story.

CHAPTER 6:

BROTHERS

At that time, all I wanted was peace in our home, for my mom to be healthy, and for my dad to have better days. But all I had ever seen were negative streets and broken paths. This was the world I lived in—where we went shopping, and where my Grandma Maria lived. After months of staying at the Townhouse Motel, we finally moved into an apartment at the Tangerine Hill Apartments. For the first time, I saw the "better side" of town. This new home, a 200-unit complex, was across the tracks, far from the railroad, and I got to attend one of the best schools in the city.

Around this time, I learned I was going to have a younger brother. The news excited me. Finally, I would have someone to talk to, to play with, and to show off. When my brother Enrique (Henry) was born, he was the first baby I had ever held. I remember how my heart melted, and I felt so important holding this little soul. For years, I rocked him to sleep in a wooden chair we had, and each time his head would slump onto my shoulder, or his tiny heartbeat brushed my skin, I felt a love I had never known before. It was in those moments I built a deep connection with him. Henry gave me purpose. I wanted to be a good role model, providing him with the love and affection I so desperately longed for from our parents.

In many ways, Henry gave me what I craved—love, belonging, and validation. His simple gestures as a baby made me feel smart, able, and important. But life wasn't easy. We shared the same room, and when I had school, his cries would keep me up all night. Meanwhile, my parents' fights grew more intense. My dad's cocaine habit worsened, and our home became a battleground. Amid the chaos, my bond with Henry became my saving grace. His laughter and innocence taught me how pure love could be, even when my world was filled with so much pain.

As Henry grew, I took it upon myself to protect him. I taught him the unspoken rules of survival in our family, hoping to shield him from the worst of our parents' dysfunction. But he was still innocent. I remember the day he told his teacher that our parents smoked marijuana, which became a big issue at home. I had to explain why we couldn't share things like that with others. He was just trying to help—he wanted our parents to be better, just like I did.

Despite everything, we found ways to laugh, wrestle, and play games that distracted us from the chaos. Then came the news that we were going to have another sibling. My mom hoped for a girl but was blessed with another boy. My youngest brother, Sammy, was born on November 9, 1995—exactly ten years and two days after me. His arrival changed me even more. Having two brothers to care for made me grow up quickly. I felt a responsibility to protect them from our father and from the harsh realities of the world. But I was still a child myself, battling my own demons.

We were still poor, and at times, I resented my parents for bringing more children into the world when they could barely take care of the family we already had. I made up games for my brothers, like shooting rolled-up socks into a laundry basket or playing football with a sock. But no matter what fun we created, my parents' anger always intruded. They'd come in, yelling, telling us we'd break something or hurt each other. I remember wanting so badly for my dad to play with us, but he'd always say "later." Later never came, and that disappointment still stings. Now, I understand that he was too hurt to be there for us, but back then, it crushed me.

To escape, I'd spend as much time outside as possible. I found friends who were like me—kids who understood what it was like to struggle. Some of them even shared food with me, since we often didn't have much at home. I was grateful for those small acts of kindness. But at the same time, everyone in the apartments knew what was happening inside our house.

They could hear my parents yelling and see the marks left from the beatings. Kids in the complex would mock me, imitating my cries or the insults my parents screamed. Eventually, I learned to stay silent when I got hit, so no one could make fun of me. I built a wall around my feelings, and it became a shield I carried for years.

Despite the chaos and danger, there were older guys who watched out for me. They'd step in when things got too rough. I remember one time, during a football game, I got pile-driven onto the concrete. I was bleeding badly. A few older guys, including my friend Joseph, carried me home. Those moments of protection gave me a sense of safety I rarely felt anywhere else. That's why I was willing to risk everything for the kind of connection we all need as humans, but that I wasn't getting at home.

It's easy to see why kids like me find solace in gangs or other harmful environments. We're all just looking for connection, for safety, for someone to love us. I see now that many of the kids I grew up with turned to gangs, drugs, or other escapes because they couldn't find love or acceptance at home. The streets became my outlet, and I learned how to fight, how to talk tough, and how to survive. I even taught my brothers these skills, hoping they wouldn't be as lost as I was.

I remember one particular run-in when some older boys cornered me. I tried to run but got caught on a fence. They beat me, and I was left hanging by my arm, hooked onto a metal spike. Thankfully, my older homies came to my rescue just in time. But that day, I realized something: in my neighborhood, you either learned to be tough, or you got eaten alive.

I didn't start out wanting to be tough. But with everything going on, my way of coping was to become the 'badass' everyone feared. For a while, I enjoyed the attention. At school and at home, I was already seen as the bad kid, so why not embrace it? The older guys and I watched movies like 'American Me' and 'Blood In Blood Out,' imagining ourselves as the tough guys we saw on screen. We gave each other tattoos with staples and hung out in the fields, smoking weed and planning small-time missions where we would scheme to get money. It felt like the only way out for people like us.

I never wanted my brothers to see me weak, though. I loved them too much for that. But deep inside, I was breaking. I was caught between wanting to protect them and knowing I wasn't strong enough to fix our situation. They gave me hope, but I didn't yet have the strength to heal myself.

Deep down, I felt broken and wanted to scream for help. But when I spent time with my brothers, those moments were some of my best memories—even today. My brothers taught me that I wasn't a bad person and that I could love and be loved. I had to teach them everything—how to throw a ball, how to catch, how to play sports. I wanted them to have everything I had wished for as a child. But it was hard when we were still dealing with parents who were falling deeper into their own problems. My parents didn't know how to have healthy conversations, so their fights only got worse, and we were always the bystanders, forced to watch. I did my best to distract my brothers from all the chaos, trying to shield them from the same pain I was carrying.

I prayed with all my heart that they wouldn't have to suffer the way I did. I wanted to spare them from the emotional and physical pain our parents inflicted on me. But the hardest part was knowing that I couldn't take them out of our situation, no matter how much I wanted to.**

"If I destroy you, I destroy myself. If I honor you, I honor myself. "
—**Hunbatz Men, Mayan**

I was lost in this life until I understood what unconditional love was. Loving someone and being loved back is the most powerful medicine in the world. But here's the hard part: sometimes, the people who are supposed to love us—our parents, our guardians—are struggling too much with their own pain to give us the love we need.

My little brothers, Henry and Sammy, taught me what love could feel like. I was their big brother, but they saved me more than I could ever save them. Being their protector gave me a sense of purpose, even in the middle of the storm that was our family life.

Reflection/Practice:

Take a moment to think about the relationships in your life that have shaped you, especially those with your siblings, family, or those you've tried to protect. What did these relationships teach you about love, responsibility, and sacrifice? Did you ever feel torn between wanting to be strong for others but feeling weak inside?

Now, reflect on the love you give to others. Write down how those connections have helped you heal or hurt. If you've ever felt responsible for protecting someone, think about how that role influenced your own growth.

Finally, practice compassion for yourself. Understand that even when you're the one giving love, it's important to receive it, too. You don't have to carry the weight of everyone's pain by yourself. Compassion is a tool, not just for others but for you as well. It's okay to be vulnerable—it's where real strength comes from. In this understanding, find the space to honor yourself, just as you honor those you've protected.

CHAPTER 7:

ROSES GROWING IN THE CONCRETE

Growing up in a small town like Sanger, California, it was impossible not to notice the divisions in the city—the stark contrast between the "haves" and the "have-nots." The train tracks along Academy Avenue symbolized more than just a geographic divide; they were a boundary between two worlds. On one side were the wealthier areas, with manicured lawns, cleaner streets, and access to resources like supermarkets and doctors' offices. On the other side of the tracks lay neighborhoods where poverty was ingrained in the soil—where gang activity was prevalent, liquor stores outnumbered grocery stores, and survival, not prosperity, was the goal.

In Sanger, the Bulldogs and Sureños carved out their territories, with the train tracks marking the line between them. This divide wasn't just about gangs; it was about a deeper separation—of opportunity, security, and belonging. The further you lived from the tracks, the better your chances of experiencing the illusion of a "normal" life. But for those of us growing up on the wrong side of town, it didn't matter if you were Bulldog or Sureño. The reality was the same: poverty, violence, and limited options.

As a Mexican-American child, living in Sanger felt like being trapped in a pre-written story—a narrative where jail, addiction, or early death seemed inevitable. But this isn't just a Sanger story; it's a universal story for many of us born into underprivileged communities. No matter the city or the name of the gang, the root causes are the same: generational poverty, systemic violence, and the oppression of entire communities.

I saw it firsthand—kids like me, joining gangs, not just because of peer pressure, but because gangs filled a void. They gave us a sense of belonging when the world around us made us feel like we didn't belong anywhere. They provided a family structure we lacked at home. But joining a gang also meant adopting a new identity, compromising our morals, and risking everything. For many of us, the need for acceptance outweighed the cost of our safety and well-being.

By the time I was in fifth grade, I saw how my friends on the streets knew how to hustle, and I wanted to learn. But by then, the cops had started cracking down with gang injunctions, using every excuse to arrest us. Tattoos, colors, even where we lived—everything was a target. If you got caught, the new laws ensured you'd serve extra time. The system was designed to keep us down, to trap us in the very neighborhoods we were trying to escape.

It wasn't until later that I learned about redlining, a practice that dates back to the 1930s. Redlining wasn't just about dividing cities; it was about keeping certain people—Black, Brown, Indigenous, and other non-white communities—out of wealthier areas. Redlining made it impossible for us to get loans, buy homes, or build any form of generational wealth. Our neighborhoods, already impoverished, were left to rot while wealthier areas thrived. It's systemic racism, baked into the very foundation of the cities we live in.

As a kid, I didn't understand how all this—poverty, racism, and lack of education—would shape my life. I thought our struggles were because of my parents' personal failures. I didn't know then that the deck was stacked against them from the beginning. My father's choices weren't just bad decisions; they were survival tactics, the only way he knew how to navigate a system that was designed to see him fail.

I didn't want my brothers to grow up in this reality. I wanted to protect them from the world, to give them a better life than the one I had. But how could I do that when I was still struggling to survive myself? I didn't have the tools, the knowledge, or the emotional stability to show them a different path. All I could do was try to be there for them, to teach them what little I knew about life.

"They tried to bury us. They didn't know we were seeds."
—Dinos Christianopoulos

"Walk like you have 10,000 ancestors walking behind you"
—Unknown

My message to you, if you're still living in the barrio, the hood, or whatever it's called in your city, is this: you have the power to change your story. You don't have to follow the path that's been laid out for you by poverty, gangs, or systemic oppression. Start by educating yourself—learn about redlining, learn about your civil rights, and understand the history of how our neighborhoods were intentionally set up to keep us from succeeding. When you understand the system, you can start to break free from it.

If you want to honor your ancestors, don't kill each other over streets and colors that were never meant to define us. Our grandparents and great-grandparents fought, bled, and died for us to have the opportunities we do today. We owe it to them— and to ourselves—to rise above the violence and the hate.

As a child, I blamed my parents for our struggles, not understanding the bigger picture. But as I've grown, I've come to realize that their pain was rooted in a system that devalued them from the start. My father wasn't just making bad decisions; he was doing the best he could with the cards he was dealt. This doesn't excuse his actions, but it helps me understand the generational pain that was passed down to him, and that he unknowingly passed down to us.

I challenge you to take up the mantle of leadership in your community. Don't destroy your neighborhood with guns, drugs, and violence. Instead, educate yourself and those around you. Teach the younger generation about financial literacy, civil rights, and how to build generational wealth. Start working out every day—keep your body and mind strong. Share your feelings with people you trust or write them down. Most importantly, help the younger ones who don't have role models. Be the change that your community needs.

Reflection/Practice:

Think about the neighborhood you grew up in, or the one you live in now. What are the invisible barriers—like poverty, gang violence, or systemic racism—that have shaped your community? How have they impacted your life and the lives of those around you?

Now, think about what it would mean to break those barriers. What steps can you take to start healing your community? How can you become a leader, not just for yourself, but for the younger generation looking up to you?

Write down your thoughts and reflections. What has the barrio taught you about survival? What can you teach the barrio about thriving?

CHAPTER 8:

FAMILY PAIN

I was in my room, listening to music and wrestling with my brothers, like we always did for fun. Out of nowhere, my dad burst in, yelling at me, telling me I was a bad influence on them. I tried to explain I was just listening to music, but before I could say anything more, he rushed at me. He grabbed me by the throat, slammed me onto the bed, and started choking me. My brothers stood frozen, watching. I remember looking at them, trying with all my strength to break free. My mom rushed in and pulled him off of me. I was angry—angry because I was never good enough for him. Anything I enjoyed, he would tear down and say it was bad, and too often, that would turn physical. After this incident, my mom sent me to stay with my grandmother for a few weeks.

At my grandmother's house, I didn't tell her what had happened, but she told me I needed to respect my dad because the Bible says so. I hated that I couldn't be real with anyone. Religion was always there, casting a shadow, making me feel like I was the problem, like I was bad. It's the same reason my mom stayed with my dad for so long—religion kept telling her she had to, that it was her duty. No one knew what went on inside our home, and my mom never spoke about it. I could see the toll it took on her, even as a child. She carried the weight of depression and loneliness, even though she didn't know how to name it then. It hurt me because I saw she needed help, but we were trapped, with no way out.

Living with my Abuela Nina during that time built up resentment in me. This was a few years before my Abuelo Pascual passed away, and I could see he was struggling too. He would walk the halls, talking to himself, sometimes completely disconnected from reality. My grandmother turned to religion as a way to heal the trauma we were all living through, but it wasn't enough. My uncles were either caught up in their own lives or too deep into their drug use to help. It felt like my mom and I had no one to turn to. We were lost, confused, and stuck.

That's when I started drinking. Alcohol was easy to get—I saw my dad and my nino always drinking, and it seemed like the way to escape. We all drank to forget, but the next day, the same problems were waiting for us. I had no healthy outlets, and the bonds with my extended family were practically nonexistent. My school labeled me the "bad kid," and the gangs and drugs were always there, tempting me, offering a false sense of belonging. My dad, being the youngest of seven brothers, was always the favorite uncle. When I tried to speak up, to talk to his side of the family, they dismissed me, said we were liars, or that we must have done something to deserve his anger. There was no escaping the trauma—it had been with me since birth, and there was no end in sight.

I watched my mom suffer, day in and day out. She cooked, cleaned, and tried her best to please my dad, but he ridiculed her, neglected her, and at times, physically abused her. I began to see why she spoke so negatively about herself, why her mental health was deteriorating. She loved deeply, but it seemed like all she got in return was pain. I hated how people treated her in public, judging her without knowing the battles she was fighting at home. Neighbors and friends looked down on her, thinking they were better. But they had no idea. If only she had someone to talk to, someone who could hear her and understand her.

Looking back now, I see that my mom was incredibly strong. She didn't let the gossip or judgment get to her, always telling me that what others said didn't matter. But I wonder—was that resilience or just a way to cope? Society throws around the word "resilience," but it's more than just enduring. Resilience is a survival skill, but healing—that's what we need to truly live, to feel joy, and to connect with the world. Healing transforms us, allowing us to break free from the cycle of suffering.

Children who grow up in environments like mine are wired to see the world as dangerous. We're taught to survive, not to thrive. To transform that mindset, you have to understand where the suffering comes from. Only then can you begin to change, to build a path toward healing. It takes time, patience, and a lot of compassion for yourself. You have to learn to forgive, to let go of the judgment, and to understand that setbacks will happen.

As my mom started to find her voice and get out of the house more, she had her third child, my baby brother, Sammy. Our family grew, and so did the community around us. I saw firsthand how gentrification worked in our neighborhood. Friends who had moved into new houses suddenly stopped being friends, while those who stayed behind in the apartments would steal from the ones who had moved on. The new housing developments brought change—some good, some bad—but it made me realize how much division exists based on class and where you live.

By the time I reached sixth grade, my behavior was spiraling out of control. I knew we were poor, and I wasn't accepted for who I was. Even when I tried, my teachers couldn't see past their biases. I won a multiplication test against my teacher, and she accused me of cheating. I hadn't cheated. I was good at math, but that didn't matter. Later, I copied a friend's homework because I had forgotten to do mine, and my teacher used it as an excuse to call me a cheater again. She called my parents, spreading her biases without understanding my situation. It wasn't that I didn't want to do my homework—I was just so tired from taking care of my brothers that sometimes I fell asleep before I could finish it.

As my parents' fights continued, I used humor to hide my pain. When that didn't work, I turned to anger. Anger became my shield, a way to protect myself from the hurt I didn't know how to handle. My arguments with my mom became more frequent. Sometimes, she would hit me until she passed out, and I would have to revive her with alcohol. After years of physical and emotional abuse, I became numb. I laughed when people yelled at me, egging them on, daring them to hit me. Pain became something I could endure, but it also built walls between me and the people I loved.

I found moments of escape with my brothers. We'd go to the store, buy chips with food stamps, and play video games at the pizza parlor. The manager, Jim, would sometimes give us extra quarters or pizza. Those little acts of kindness meant the world to us. Jim was someone I could talk to, someone who didn't judge me. He just listened.

At the time, I didn't understand that my parents and grandparents were struggling with their own traumas. They were judged, shamed, and belittled for not speaking English well, for being poor. That pain shaped them, and they passed it on to us without even realizing it. They didn't know any other way.

"Just imagine becoming the way you used to be as a very young child, before you understood the meaning of any word, before opinions took over your mind. The real you is loving, joyful, and free. The real you is just like a flower, just like the wind, just like the ocean, just like the sun."

—Don Miguel Ruiz

—————————

Reflection/Practice:

To heal the false narratives we've been told and reclaim the love for ourselves in a world that sometimes pushes us to forget our worth, try the following practice. This exercise will help you nurture self-compassion while addressing deeper wounds from childhood trauma.

Find a quiet, comfortable space: Sit in a position that allows you to be both alert and relaxed. Take a few deep breaths to ground yourself and settle your mind.

Breathe in healing, breathe out compassion: With each inhale, imagine the air bringing warmth, healing, and light into your heart space. As you exhale, visualize sending out compassion and love, not only toward yourself but to the world. Repeat out loud or in your mind:

"May I be happy. May I be peaceful. May I be free from suffering."

Feel the compassion expanding inside you with each breath. Reconnect with your inner child: Now, take a moment to reflect on a difficult experience from your childhood—something that still lingers in your heart. Picture yourself as the child you were in that moment, the child who wasn't protected, loved, or understood. Look deeply at that child and say,

"It wasn't your fault. You are worthy of love. You are sacred."

Offer healing to your inner child: Imagine embracing that younger version of yourself, offering the comfort and protection you needed at that time. Speak the words of love and support you wish you had heard back then.

"You are loved. You are enough. You deserve to be seen and cherished."

Conclude with self-compassion: Return to the present moment. Once again, breathe deeply. Inhale the warmth of healing and exhale compassion, knowing that you are on the journey to reclaiming your wholeness. You are worthy of love and peace. Whenever feelings of guilt, shame, or self-doubt arise, repeat this practice to remind yourself that healing is a process, and you deserve every bit of it.

CHAPTER 9:

MIDDLE SCHOOL

During junior high (seventh and eighth grade), it often felt like my teachers were out to get me, as if their mission was to push me out of school. I would walk into class knowing that referrals were already written for me and my friends before we even sat down. Some teachers went as far as making me stand in front of the room, working on the board like some sort of spectacle. Others seemed obsessed with catching us out, egging us on just enough so that we'd react and end up in the principal's office. It was a cycle—one that felt like a game I couldn't win. These teachers thought that fear would teach us, that discipline and shame would somehow fix our behavior. What they didn't understand was that fear only shuts down learning, especially when you're already dealing with the kind of chaos I was.

The truth was, no one at school could hurt me more than my parents already had. So, I built a defense—a mindset that made me feel invincible, a shield to ensure no one could scar me the way my parents did. But that shield came at a cost. I became hardened, quick to fight, and unable to connect with people unless they carried the same pain. Ego became my armor, but it also cut me off from the parts of myself that needed healing.

School became a game of survival. I mastered being the "bad" student, but I made sure to get good grades because I didn't want to deal with getting whooped at home. There was this one teacher who played into the game more than anyone. I remember being so close to an A, sitting at 89 percent, and I asked for the grade bump. He refused and gave me a B. That moment solidified my hatred for school, for the system. It was the first time I realized that the educational system wasn't built for kids like me—for Mexican-American kids, for anyone from poverty. We were seen as problems, not people. But what no one saw was that our shared suffering was our connection. We weren't bad kids; we were kids navigating a world that didn't understand our pain.

Not all teachers were like that, though. Mr. Wright was one of the few who saw me. He made history come alive, dressed up as historical figures, and showed us how we were products of our past. He had expectations of me, but they were fair, and they made me feel like he believed in me. He made me understand that if we don't learn from our past, we're doomed to repeat it. Mr. Wright connected with me in a way that no other teacher did, and that connection kept me grounded.

At that age, I thought I had the world figured out. I wasn't going to let anyone see what I was really feeling—how much I was struggling inside. By then, I had built up walls so high around my pain that I didn't let anyone in. The teachers who tried to break me down only made those walls stronger. They judged me for how I was coping with life without ever knowing what I had been through, what I went through every single day.

In middle school, the world starts to expect you to grow up overnight. For some of us, especially kids of color dealing with poverty and trauma, we're already living adult lives. We're expected to survive in a world that's trying to define us before we even understand who we are. If you don't have the right support, if you don't have anyone to talk to, it's easy to feel alone, isolated, even suicidal during these years. Trying to navigate all of this, while being a person of color in a society that constantly tries to tell you who you should be, is a battle not everyone sees.

The one bright spot during this time was meeting my comrade, David Vera. He lived in the apartments next to mine, and on the first day of middle school, we walked home together. I knew of him from sports, but that day I got to know him. He made me laugh, and for the first time in a long time, I felt like I had someone who truly understood me. Our bond became my lifeline during those years.

By the time you leave middle school, you're fourteen, just four years away from adulthood. These are critical years to find support, to explore, to figure out who you are and what you want. Take part in anything that takes you outside the box you're used to—clubs, field trips, sports. For some of us, it's the first time we'll see a beach or a museum, or a city that's more than fifty miles away. Exposing yourself to different opportunities shows you that there's more to the world than just the hood you're growing up in. And if you make mistakes, learn from them. Only make the same mistake once, because if you don't, those mistakes can become habits that are harder to break.

"Everybody is a genius. But if you judge a fish by its ability to climb a tree, it will live its whole life believing that it is stupid.
—Albert Einstein

Middle school is your chance to decide how you want to live in this world and what you want your story to be. For me, it was a time when I felt the weight of everything—being poor, being Mexican, feeling stuck in a system that wasn't made for me. By the time I entered school, I had learned to be ashamed of my culture, my language, my heritage. I felt like society saw me as nothing more than a gangster or a troublemaker, and with no other guidance, I became what everyone expected me to be.

But reflecting now, I realize how much middle school shaped me. It was a time when I could have gone down so many paths. Only two teachers saw my potential, and it was their belief in me that kept me from falling completely into the expectations society had placed on me. So many kids across the country are still going through this—fitting into a mold that doesn't see their humanity. Schools can change this narrative, but it takes early intervention, compassion, and a focus on transforming suffering within the mind, body, and soul.

CHAPTER 10:

LOYALTY

David Vera became my brother, and I loved being in his company. He was more than just a friend; he was someone I could trust, someone who saw me for who I was without judgment or shame. David always wanted the best for me, using his love to lift me up, not tear me down. Raised by his dad, who he called Pap, and his Tio Mundo, David came from a strong family unit that welcomed me as one of their own. His older brother, Fabian, known as Fave (or *The Fave One*, as he liked to say), and his sister, Tencha, were also a big part of my life. Tencha would lace David with new clothes, and in turn, he would pass his old fits down to me. Seeing the way they took care of each other, I knew I wanted to be that kind of older sibling for my brothers.

David introduced me to a world I had never experienced before. Through him, I soaked up culture and learned about music—hip hop, graffiti, and street art. Though I never became a skater like David, who was phenomenal on a board, I did my best to keep up with him around town. David "put me up on game," teaching me about everything from Wu-Tang Clan to Nas, from Mac Dre to The Fugees. In those days, it felt like I was always at his house, or we were out finding ways to stay away from home. At David's house, I had an escape—a place where I could breathe, laugh, and feel like myself.

At home, it was chaos. My parents' unhealthy relationship and the weight of their own childhood trauma followed them everywhere they went, always ready to explode. I had two amazing brothers, but I felt trapped in that house. So I would sneak out, telling my little brother Henry that I was heading to McDonald's and would bring him something back if he promised not to tell. Sometimes I could follow through if I had money, but more often than not, I'd come up with an excuse because I didn't have any extra cash. The truth was, I just needed to get away.

David's house was a sanctuary for me. We would watch movies, practice graffiti, play basketball, skate, and talk about life. It was therapy, the kind I didn't know I needed. David's dad and Tio Mundo were boxing trainers, and they taught me how to channel my anger into something constructive—how to throw a punch, how to focus. David himself was a Golden Glove champion, and in their house, there was structure and discipline, but it was all rooted in care and love. They became the authority figures I could respect because they didn't come at me with anger or judgment. They had rules, but they also had compassion. It was the balance I had never experienced at home.

The more time I spent with David and Jose Guzman, another close friend, the more we became inseparable. We built our identity around each other, finding a brotherhood that gave me hope and direction when I had none. School, on the other hand, felt pointless. I only went to meet up with the homies and figure out what we were doing afterward. The teachers, administrators, and even the campus security seemed to have one mission—to kick me out. And as much as they tried to catch me out and punish me, I couldn't help but wish they had also tried to show me some compassion and understanding. We need more people in schools who understand how powerful connection and empathy can be in helping someone transform their pain.

At home, things didn't get any better. My parents continued to make the same mistakes, disrespecting their bodies, relationships, and us as their children. I began sneaking out more often, meeting up with David or Jose. We'd stay out late, sometimes stealing from cars, driving Jose's mom's rental around town, or getting into trouble just for fun. Graffiti became an outlet for us, a way to express ourselves in a world that didn't seem to care about us.

One night, David and I were invited to a party by a girl he was talking to at the time. We were excited, not realizing the tension that would follow. The party was on the other side of town, where people weren't always welcoming to outsiders. We weren't gang bangers, just kids looking to have fun, but we were naïve to the rules of the streets. After a few hours of hanging out, someone asked, "What do you bang?" That's when everything changed. Suddenly, there were twelve guys surrounding us, ready to start something.

David stood by my side without hesitation. For the first time in my life, I felt someone standing firmly with me, refusing to leave. He was loyal. As the situation escalated, the girl we were with pulled us inside just in time, walking us to a van where someone offered to drive us out of there. But as we drove off, we were surrounded again. The van driver told us he couldn't take us far, only up the street. Once we reached the stop sign, David and I had no choice but to get out and run.

For some reason, I couldn't move that night. I was weighed down, both physically and emotionally. I told David to run without me, but he refused. "You run, or we stay here together," he said. And that's when I knew—I had to run. We jumped a fence as bullets sprayed, hiding in a backyard until it was safe. Eventually, we made it home, but that night stayed with me forever. It was the first of many dangerous nights for years to come for me.

"Peace has never come from dropping bombs. Real peace comes from enlightenment and educating people to behave in a divine manner."
—Carlos Santana

That night cemented the loyalty and love David had for me. His loyalty wasn't just about being by my side physically—it was about standing with me in the hardest moments. If you have a friend like that, never forget to remind them how much you love and value them. True friendship, like David's, is rare, and it should be cherished.

When negative thoughts or emotions weigh you down, you can find healing by drawing on the loyalty and wisdom of those who care about you. Here's a practice to help you stay connected to that love, even in tough times:

Think of a person who has provided you with love, wisdom, and understanding—a friend, sibling, cousin, or even a mentor.

Reflect on something that's been bothering you lately. Now, imagine the advice you would give that person if they were going through what you're going through. Write it down as if you're writing to them.

Take a few deep breaths in and out. As you breathe, imagine offering love and compassion to that person (or even to yourself).

Now, write a letter of advice to yourself, using the same love and care you would give to someone else. Be honest and gentle with yourself.

Read the letter out loud, and whenever negative thoughts or feelings come up, return to those words to ground and comfort you.

Repeat this practice as often as needed—whether it's daily, weekly, or whenever life feels overwhelming.

By practicing loyalty to yourself and those you love, you build a foundation of strength that will carry you through even the toughest moments.

CHAPTER 11:

HIP HOP

Growing up on 2Pac, he became my inspiration and role model. His music spoke directly to my soul, and I believed that one day I could change lives and mindsets the same way he did—except I'd do it with my newfound knowledge and awareness. Even though I didn't have the privilege of attending public school for many years, I felt like I was getting educated through the books I read and the music I absorbed. Music, especially hip-hop, became my classroom. But it didn't erase the struggles I was still dealing with at home—my parents fighting, protecting my little brothers, and trying to fit in at school. I remember listening to 2Pac's song *Changes* every morning before school. It was my anthem because it reflected the same struggles I saw at home, in school, and in the streets.

Artists like 2Pac, Wu-Tang, Nas, Outkast, and UGK hit me on a deep level. They described the world the way I saw it but couldn't yet explain. Through their words, I found guidance when I had none. Hip-hop became my lifeline, and these artists gave me a sense of belonging, showing me that the challenges I faced weren't mine alone. They helped me understand the injustice, racism, hate, and power dynamics that were playing out in front of me. It was 2Pac who helped me see the deep-seated anger many people of color and those in poverty carry inside.

The Hate U Give Little Infants Fucks Everybody —THUG LIFE—was something 2Pac said that I could relate to once I began learning more about the history of oppression, redlining, and the mistreatment that non-white populations have faced for generations. Once I learned this, I knew I wanted to make a difference in my world. But the problem was, I didn't yet know how.

The more I immersed myself in hip-hop, the more I realized that these artists weren't just making music—they were making a difference for their people, their culture. People like GURU from Gang Starr taught me to stay sharp, strong, and clever, both mentally and physically. He showed me that it was cool to be yourself without getting caught up in drugs or self-destruction. Hip-hop wasn't just entertainment—it was a guide, teaching me life lessons that I wasn't learning at home or in school.

At this time, my home life was spiraling downhill fast. The only thing that kept me grounded was music and art. Hip-hop helped me see the world clearly, while graffiti gave me an outlet to express what was bottled up inside. It was through these forms of expression that I reclaimed control over my life. Graffiti, in particular, gave me confidence. I created a name for myself— *EPIK* . To me, it was a statement that no matter what people thought of me or my abilities, I would live my life in an epic way before I died. I didn't know graffiti well at first, but I wanted to be part of a crew called Y2K, and their style was out of this world. Eventually, I started rolling with them.

Having never felt like I belonged anywhere, joining the crew gave me a sense of power and protection that I had longed for. I finally had status, reputation, and a name that people recognized. It wasn't just about tagging walls—it was about claiming my place in a world that had tried to push me to the margins.

"Hip-hop has different elements dealing with music, rap, graffiti art, B-boys (what you call break boys) … And also dealing with culture, and a whole movement dealing with wisdom and understanding, as well as peace, unity, and fun."

—Afrika Bambaataa

———————

For the first time in my life, I had found power, a voice, and a way to express myself. After years of feeling powerless, worthless, and voiceless, hip-hop and graffiti changed all that. I remember walking around with my case of CDs, always looking for a place to pump my music and vibe out. I tagged *EPIK* everywhere because it symbolized how I wanted to live my life, regardless of the struggles I faced. Hip-hop and graffiti saved my life because they connected me with others who were trying to understand the world, just like I was. They gave me the wisdom— *the game* —that I wasn't getting anywhere else.

Here's a playlist of songs that helped me understand the struggle of poverty and also gave me the inspiration to keep pushing forward:

- *My Block* by 2Pac
- *Changes* by 2Pac
- *Nothing to Lose* by 2Pac
- *Me Against the World* by 2Pac
- *Hold on Be Strong* by 2Pac
- Smile *by Scarface (featuring 2Pac)*
- They Don't Give a F *** About Us* by 2Pac*
- Face the World *by Nipsey Hussle*
- The Weather *by Nipsey Hussle, Rick Ross, Cuzzy Capone*
- *How Long Can it Last* by UGK
- I Can *by Nas*

- *Warrior Song* by Nas
- *My Advice 2 You* by Gang Starr
- *Impossible* by Wu-Tang
- *A Better Tomorrow* by Wu-Tang
- *All That I Got is You* by Ghostface Killah
- *If I Ruled the World (Imagine That)* by Nas (featuring Lauryn Hill)
- *Revolutionary Warfare* by Nas (featuring Lake)
- *Classic* by MED, Talib Kweli
- *Corner Store* by Planet Asia, Calvin Valentine
- *Doo-Wop (That Thing)* by Lauryn Hill
- *Appletree* by Erykah Badu
- *On and On* by Erykah Badu
- *Git Up, Git Out* by Outkast (featuring Goodie Mob)
- *Sugar Hill* by AZ
- *As We Enter* by Damian Marley (featuring Nas)
- *Patience* by Damian Marley (featuring Nas)
- *Concrete Jungle* by Bob Marley
- *Don't Put Me Down (If I'm Brown)* by El Chicano
- *Jefe De Jefes* by Los Tigres Del Norte
- *Vida Peligrosa* by Arsenal Efectivo

For the first time in my life, I had found power, a voice, and a way to express myself. After years of feeling powerless, worthless, and voiceless, hip-hop and graffiti changed all that. I remember walking around with my case of CDs, always looking for a place to pump my music and vibe out. I tagged *EPIK* everywhere because it symbolized how I wanted to live my life, regardless of the struggles I faced. Hip-hop and graffiti saved my life because they connected me with others who were trying to understand the world, just like I was. They gave me the wisdom— *the game* —that I wasn't getting anywhere else.

Just like hip-hop gave me a way to find my voice and express my pain, you can tap into your own experiences and turn them into something powerful. Here's a practice that can help you channel your feelings and find your own voice when you feel lost or overwhelmed:

Reflection/Practice:

Find a Safe Space: Whether it's through music, art, or writing, create a space where you can fully express yourself without judgment. Play a song that speaks to you or grab a pen and start writing out what you're feeling.

Reflect on Your Struggle: Think about the challenges you're facing right now. Are there parallels to what your role models or favorite artists talk about in their work? Let those connections give you the courage to confront your own pain.

Create Your Own Beat: Just like how hip-hop artists turn their struggles into lyrics, try writing down what's bothering you in the form of a poem, rap, or even a letter to yourself. Use your words as a way to get it out.

Express Through Art: If writing isn't your thing, try art. Whether it's drawing, painting, or tagging, express yourself in a way that feels authentic to you. Let your creativity be your outlet.

Stay True to Your Voice: Don't let anyone else define who you are or how you should express yourself. Hip-hop taught me that your voice matters, and it's important to stay true to who you are, no matter what the world tries to tell you.

By embracing your struggles and expressing them creatively, you can find power and healing, just like I did. Let your voice be heard, and don't be afraid to live epic.

CHAPTER 12:

HOMELESSNESS

My dad was using more cocaine than ever—or maybe I was just noticing it more. He and I never had a close relationship, and during this time, our conflict grew worse. He tried to control my mom and me, and when that didn't work, he'd get mean and hit us. This had been my reality for as long as I could remember, but it was starting to take a serious toll on my mind, body, and soul. One morning during football season, I wanted to go see a high school game across the street at Tom Flores Stadium. My dad called me a dumbass for wanting to go. It was nothing new—he always used his control and intimidation to keep me in check. That night, I stayed in my room, upset, wishing that my parents were different and that my brothers and I didn't have to live this life. I lay there, listening to 2Pac's *Changes* on repeat, letting the words sink into my spirit. The next day, I woke up determined to make a change for my family.

When I came downstairs, I could hear my parents arguing. The smell of beans and papas filled the air, a scent that still brings back memories of that day every time I smell it. I walked into the kitchen with a new energy, and in that moment, I blamed my dad for all our suffering. I believed he was the reason my mom had been on disability since 1989. I thought all the hurt he caused her was why her body was breaking down. That morning, I decided to confront him. I told him he was a coward and a pathetic excuse for a father and a man. I said people like 2Pac would beat his ass for all the bullshit he put us through. My dad called me a "p***y" and said I didn't know what being a man meant. I looked him dead in the eyes and said, "It takes one to know one."

Before I knew it, he lost his mind and charged at me. But this time, I was ready. I anticipated the grab, slipped through, and started swinging with all the hate I had bottled up for him. He stumbled onto the couch, and I kept swinging, not stopping until my mom screamed for me to quit. My little brothers were watching, and as I stopped, for the first time in my life, I felt like I had won. But it was a hollow victory because my dad told me to "get the fuck out" or he was going to call the cops.

That day changed everything. The sound of my mom and brothers crying still echoes in my mind. My mom didn't leave with me, and that hurt more than I can put into words. I felt abandoned, betrayed, and alone. It was in that moment that I stopped trusting people. It felt like doing the right thing didn't matter, and I couldn't rely on anyone, not even my own family.

Being kicked out forced me to take control of my own life, whether I was ready or not. My parents didn't come looking for me, and I was on my own. With so much hate and misdirection, I quickly found myself getting into trouble, experimenting with hard drugs, and going down a path of crime and violence. By the time I was fifteen, I was doing crank, cocaine, acid, and smoking weed daily to numb the pain. I thought I was grown, doing what I needed to survive.

At first, I bounced from one friend's house to another, but there were nights when no one could take me in, and I had to sleep in the park. I'd walk the streets until I got so tired that I'd lay down on a park slide and wait for the sun to come up. I dodged cops, always on the lookout, knowing they'd take me in if they found me out past curfew.

Selling drugs and getting high became my way of surviving. I was labeled a "bad kid" by society, but no one understood that I was just doing what I had to do to get by. School had kicked me out, and I figured the streets were my only option. I thought being "hood rich" was the answer. I knew there was a chance I'd end up in jail or worse, but at the time, it seemed like my only shot at escaping poverty.

What hurt the most about being homeless wasn't just not having a place to sleep—it was the realization that I had no family to turn to. My dad had turned his family against me, making them believe I was the problem, that I was the one destroying the family. My Grandma Maria, who I had always adored, told me she didn't want to see me unless I apologized to my dad. I was heartbroken. All I ever wanted was to hug her, eat *pan dulce* , and water her plants like I used to. But now, I was cut off from my roots, and I had no one.

After being kicked out, I started crashing at a friend's house whose mom worked nights. His older brother was part of a graffiti crew we all admired, and their house was a place of freedom. There was no judgment. You could express yourself, and that felt like a gift. But even there, my stay was temporary, and eventually, I was asked to move on. It felt like I was always overstaying my welcome wherever I went, no matter how hard I tried to be invisible.

I was exhausted—physically and emotionally—always trying to find a place to stay, feeling like a burden wherever I went. I wanted to cry, to give up. I was masking my pain with drugs and the status I was building in the streets, but deep down, I was falling apart. Days like this I just want to run! Run so far that no one can ever see or catch up to me.

I hate when life makes me feel defeated. It hurts so bad mybrain cells depleted. From trying to find connections that simply do not spark, but knowing life can be different deep within my heart. At times I feel that I do not know what it is I must do, in order to see this world through. A multitude of tragedies spread all across the world. Maybe from greed, but purely from evil. They say the world has lost its meaning, stuck trying to be someone else, our souls accustomed to the demeaning. The universe holds so much mystics. We are too blind, brainwashed to be zombies and statistics. Some say I'm misguided; living in a sphere that I see is meticulously divided. Days like this I just can't hide it. I feel I can change—I just got to fight it. The temptation to fit the mold, I need more compassion for my soul So, I have more love as I grow old. It's up to me to find the way because I have nowhere to run, Nowhere to hide. Just sitting in the present moment Learning to let my love and light shine.—Felipe Mercado, Poem written senior year

Reflection/Practice:

Homelessness strips you down to your core. It's not just about not having a place to sleep—it's about feeling like you don't belong anywhere, like there's no safe space for you in the world. The weight of that can crush your spirit if you let it. But here's the thing: even when the world feels like it's falling apart, there's still a light inside of you. You have to find it, hold on to it, and let it guide you.

Here's a practice that helped me reconnect with myself when I felt lost:

Find a quiet space: Whether you're outside, in a room, or even just sitting alone in your car, find a place where you can be with your thoughts.

Breathe deeply: Close your eyes and take slow, deep breaths. As you breathe in, imagine you're filling your lungs with light and hope. As you breathe out, release all the pain and hurt you're carrying.

Reflect on your journey: Think about where you are now and how far you've come. Acknowledge the pain, the struggles, and the losses—but also recognize the strength it took to survive.

Write a letter to your past self: Imagine you're writing to the child or teenager you once were. Tell them what you wish they had known. Offer them love, compassion, and the understanding they deserved but never got.

Read it out loud: Once you've written the letter, read it to yourself. Let the words sink in. Let the healing begin.

This practice isn't a cure-all, but it's a start. It's a way to reclaim your power, to remind yourself that even in your darkest moments, you have the strength to rise. You have the power to change your story, just like I did.

CHAPTER 13:

JUVENILE HALL

One day, I was walking with a homie and David to one of his girlfriend's houses when the cops spotted us. I hadn't realized there was a warrant out for my arrest for failing to appear in court over a graffiti charge a few months back. But being homeless, there was no one to take me to court. The arresting officer saw us from afar, pulled up next to us, jumped out of his car, and said sarcastically, "Mercado, it's your lucky day! You're the next inmate going to Juvenile Hall." He acted like he was Bob Barker or Drew Carey from *The Price is Right*, but this was no game show. That day changed everything. It made it official—I was now labeled a criminal. Walking toward that squad car, I started thinking about how I'd ended up here, as if my whole life had been leading me to this point. Raised in an environment where crime was part of the fabric, I realized I had been set up for this, without even knowing it.

When I got to Juvenile Hall, the intake process was a nightmare. I had to strip naked, squat, cough—everything you see in the movies, except it was real. I felt humiliated and violated. I wanted to cry, but I held it in. After the inspection, they gave me a quick shower and a uniform. From there, I was escorted into A-unit, where I had to share a cell with another kid. This was my first taste of losing my freedom completely— couldn't use the phone when I wanted, couldn't eat when I wanted, and had to use the bathroom in front of someone else. Each day, they searched us. We only got four hours outside the cell: breakfast, lunch, dinner, and recreation, if we earned it.

My cellmate was a gang member from Fresno who'd been caught shoplifting from Mervyn's (today's Kohl's). We became good friends, passing the time by boxing, working out, and keeping each other sane. I watched the leaders of different gangs interact with each other—eating together, showing solidarity. One day, I asked why two leaders from rival hoods would get along so well. They explained that in here, your skin color was your gang. It was a harsh reality check.

After a few weeks, I was transferred to D-unit, where things were more relaxed. We had dorm-style living and could walk around, as long as we attended the mandatory school sessions. We were still on strict schedules—lights out at 9 p.m., wake-up at 7 a.m., with only set times to shower. It felt like a summer camp for trauma survivors, except the stakes were way higher.

Then, tragedy hit. A guy I had grown close to hung himself. He had just been sentenced to five years for a hit-and-run. His laughter, which I had heard just days before, was now forever silenced. His death shook me to my core. It forced me to face my own suicidal thoughts head-on. I had been ready to give up, to end it all, but watching him die made me question everything. Did I really want to go down that road? Was there another way out?

That same night, I received a letter in a purple envelope. I remember hoping it was mine as the CO handed out the mail— and it was. It was from a friend, just checking in, telling me she was thinking of me. That letter, along with one from a family who had taken me in for a while, were the only pieces of mail I received. Those letters were a lifeline. They gave me a glimpse of humanity, reminding me that someone out there cared.

Weeks passed, and I didn't get any more mail. I felt like a ghost, forgotten by the world. But those two letters—the purple envelope especially—kept me holding on. My mom visited me once before my court date. Seeing her reminded me that everyone in here was suffering. Some had lost their parents, others had been sentenced to years or life behind bars. I couldn't fathom the idea that some of these kids—these *children* —would never know life beyond the walls of Juvenile Hall. I didn't want that to be my fate.

So, I started behaving, doing everything I could to get in the COs' good graces. I wanted to be released, to have a chance to be good again. When I finally went to court, I was scared—

unsure if my parents would even show up. But they did. And when I was released, I hugged them for coming. I remember feeling a glimmer of hope, thinking maybe, just maybe, we could try to be a family. My parents took me to a small Mexican place called Jimenez, and I ate like I hadn't had real food in forever. I felt nostalgic, hopeful, and a little at peace. But I should have known better. The only reason my dad picked me up was to avoid the daily lock-up fee.

After being released, I was once again without a home. My mom lived with my grandmother, who thought I was a bad influence, and my dad was back at his mom's house, still doing drugs. I was alone again, but this time, I didn't want to go back down the path that had led me to Juvenile Hall. The experience had changed me. It made me realize I had more in me than just a desire for survival. I started questioning everything about my life and how I got here.

Unconditional love where are you?
I look everywhere, but you are not there.
Unconditional love where are you?
I need you so bad, but you are not there.
Unconditional love, tell me, does anyone really care?
I dream of safety and joy when you are near
Unconditional love please appear I yell for you, but I can't find
you here.

Unconditional love, please tell me those words I need to hear.
The words that make everything okay and take away the fear.
You know that feeling that makes you feel so alive you just want
to cheer.
Unconditional love has always been inside, not out there!

Being in the cell taught me about what I have to do inside to change what's on the outside. (Felipe Mercado in Juvenile Hall)

After being released, I was once again without a home. My mom lived with my grandmother, who thought I was a bad influence, and my dad was back at his mom's house, still doing drugs. I was alone again, but this time, I didn't want to go back down the path that had led me to Juvenile Hall. The experience had changed me. It made me realize I had more in me than just a desire for survival. I started questioning everything about my life and how I got here.

Reflection/Practice:

Being locked up strips away your freedom, but it also forces you to confront parts of yourself that you'd rather avoid. For me, it made me realize that I had been searching for unconditional love from others, when in reality, it had to start from within. Juvenile Hall taught me that I couldn't rely on the world to give me the love I needed—I had to give it to myself.

Here's a practice that helped me find that inner love when I was at my lowest:

Find a quiet space: Sit in a place where you won't be disturbed. Close your eyes and take a few deep breaths.

Reflect on your journey: Think about your life and the moments where you felt abandoned or unloved. Let yourself feel the hurt, but don't stay there.

Focus on self-compassion: Imagine yourself as the child you once were, the one who was hurt, abandoned, or neglected. Now, offer that child the unconditional love you never received. Say, "I see you. I love you. You are worthy."

Repeat these affirmations: "I am worthy of love. I am enough. I deserve to be free from suffering."

Write a letter to your past self: Tell your younger self what they needed to hear. Offer them the love and compassion they deserved but never got.

Read the letter out loud: Let the words sink into your heart. Remember that healing comes from within, and you have the power to give yourself the love you've always been seeking.

By practicing this, you can start to rebuild the parts of you that feel broken, the parts that Juvenile Hall or life's hardships may have tried to take away. True healing begins when we find the strength to love ourselves first.

CHAPTER 14:

DRUGS

"Not why the addiction, but why the pain."

—*Dr. Gabor Maté, in "Cracked Up: The Evolving Conversation—Trauma as the Root Cause of Addiction."*

After leaving Juvenile Hall, with my parents split up and my grandmother unwilling to let me live with her, I had nowhere to go. My dad was staying at Grandma Maria's house with his brother, and I ended up with them for a few months. During that time, I began experimenting with different drugs. I felt depressed, lost, and suicidal, without any tools to express my feelings. I thought drugs might offer an escape, a way to numb the pain I didn't understand. I had seen my dad, uncles, and many others take this route—using drugs to make money, to deal with the hurt, and to gain street status. Danger didn't seem like a threat because it was all I had ever known.

A part of me thought being "bad" was cool, something that would make the suffering disappear. I had been raised in an environment where being tough and reckless was celebrated. Maybe, I thought, if I became the ultimate street badass, my suffering would vanish, and I'd magically be healed.

Growing up in this world, I became adept at reading people, avoiding trouble, and surviving. But being homeless at an early age exposed me to high-risk behaviors. By age fifteen, I was using crank, cocaine, and angel dust, smoking weed daily just to manage the storm inside me. After being kicked out of school early in my freshman year, I found my way to Hallmark Charter School, an alternative education program that gave me the flexibility to meet with my teacher once a week and attend classes a few times a week. I liked this setup. My teacher was supportive, and no matter where I stayed or what my situation was, she never judged me.

Then came September 11, 2001—a day that changed everything for the country, though I barely noticed it at first. I was focused on just making it through each day. My friends and I had been hanging out at Greenwood Park before heading to class when Mr. Nidy, our art teacher, had the TV on. He started explaining what had happened and how it would impact our country. It was through his eyes that I began to understand how these larger, "macro" events affected my "micro" world.

Mr. Nidy was one of the few teachers who ever saw potential in me. He never judged me for being rough around the edges. He helped me realize that art could be an outlet for expression, and his belief in me was a lifeline I hadn't known I needed. I remember painting an African mother holding her son, and Mr. Nidy came up to me, hugged me, and told me he would always care for me, no matter what. It was the first time in my life I felt seen, that my soul mattered. It was moments like this that reminded me I was still capable of love and being loved, even in the darkest corners of my life.

Despite these glimpses of hope, drugs had already tightened their grip on me. I was deep into selling crank and eventually meth. Meth, in particular, became my ticket out—or so I thought. It was more expensive and purer than crank, and selling it gave me a way to survive, a way to make money when I had no other options. But the high never lasted, and neither did the relief from the pain I was running from.

By ninth grade, I was both using and dealing meth and marijuana. I used the money I made to buy clothes, food, and some sense of stability in an otherwise chaotic life. I even started living in the same motel I had stayed in as a child. It became my base of operations. I was living dangerously, caught in a cycle of addiction and survival.

I knew deep down that I was destroying myself, but drugs and hustling gave me a twisted sense of control. For years, I justified my actions, telling myself I was doing it for my brothers—so they wouldn't have to suffer like I had. But in reality, I was dragging them into the same darkness. I was lying to myself and to everyone around me.

One day, my world nearly came crashing down. I was driving to a mariscos restaurant with one of the biggest risk-takers I knew. We were high, drunk, and reckless, and we crashed into some trees. The car was totaled, and as we ran from the scene, I could hear the cops and helicopters closing in on us. My homie turned to me and said, "I'm turning myself in. I can't run anymore." I was stunned. I wasn't ready to face the consequences. I ran and kept running, dodging the police, helicopters overhead, and the reality that was catching up to me.

As I ran through the fields, all I could think about was not getting caught. I prayed, begging God for another chance, promising that if I made it out, I would stop dealing, stop using, and try to do good in my life. Somehow, I made it to the road, where an old-school Oldsmobile pulled up. Inside was a man who looked like an OG straight from heaven. "Get in, little homie," he said. I hesitated but got in. He told me I reminded him of himself and that these streets wouldn't offer me anything but misery. "Do good with your life," he said. "That's all I want from you." I never saw him again, but I'll never forget his words. He was the angel I didn't know I needed.

*"Heal. So we don't have another generation of trauma
passing itself off as culture."*

—Nik Jones

Drugs are often a symptom, not the cause. When people turn to drugs, it's because they are in pain—pain that society often doesn't see or care to understand. For men of color, for those growing up in trauma and poverty, drugs can feel like the only love you receive because the pain inside is too much to bear. It's a cycle that's hard to break, especially when that pain is never addressed or understood.

Addiction isn't about weakness. It's about survival. And until we start asking "Why the pain?" instead of "Why the addiction?" we will never truly heal. If you're struggling with addiction, know that there's a way out. Healing starts with understanding where the pain comes from and allowing yourself to feel it—without numbing it. Surround yourself with people who see you, who care for you, and who can help you find another way.

Here are some steps to help on the path to healing: Acknowledge the pain: It's okay to feel broken. Start by admitting that the pain is real and that it doesn't make you weak.

Find your people: Surround yourself with those who understand, who don't judge, and who want to help you heal. This could be friends, family, or a support group.

Seek safe spaces: Find places where you can be yourself without judgment—places that allow you to process your trauma and addiction with compassion.

Embrace self-compassion: Healing doesn't happen over-night. Be patient with yourself and recognize that the road to recovery is one of the greatest acts of self-love.

Ask for help: Don't be afraid to reach out when you need support. There are people out there who understand what you're going through, and they want to help.

Remember, the pain you carry doesn't have to define you. There's a way out, and it starts with acknowledging the hurt and choosing a path of healing. You are not alone in this fight.

CHAPTER 15:

SENIOR YEAR

By my senior year, I had been kicked out of school three times, spent time in Juvenile Hall, and had done every illegal drug available to me. I could barely see past my eighteenth birthday. I was convinced I'd either be dead or in jail before I graduated. Yet, deep inside, I still clung to a small hope of doing well, of not being the *travieso* everyone had labeled me. The idea that success could be the best revenge gave me a spark of resilience. Hip Hop kept me grounded. The lyrics resonated with the reality I was living, and people like David and Pennybear became the family I chose, offering me the positive energy I so desperately needed.

One person who made a profound impact on my senior year was my history teacher, Mr. Cuellar. He embraced my understanding of America's past and how it affected me, and allowed me to see history for what it really was. Another teacher, Ms. Johnstone, my English teacher, stands out just as much. She saw through my rough edges and found ways to channel my negative energy into something constructive. These two teachers did something no other adult had done in my life—they saw potential in me.

During the second semester, Ms. Johnstone gave us a scrapbook assignment that included writing five essays on topics like our first family vacation and our biggest regret. One of the prompts was about a teacher who had changed our lives. While writing, I was sure my flaws would stand out, and I would be judged. When Ms. Johnstone asked me to stay after class, my mind raced with worry. I imagined her scolding me for not meeting her standards, just like my parents used to say I was dumb and destined for failure.

But instead, she spoke with kindness. She told me she saw beyond my writing flaws and could feel the intellect and vulnerability I had put into my words. No one had ever spoken to me like that before. I broke down in tears, not because I was in trouble, but because someone finally *saw* me—really saw me.

Ms. Johnstone had a way of connecting with me, especially through our shared love of Hip Hop. When I told her how much 2Pac meant to me, she surprised me by comparing me to André 3000. I couldn't believe it—a teacher who not only understood Hip Hop but saw something special in me that even I hadn't recognized. It was as if she was unlocking a part of me I had long hidden away.

She also introduced me to the word "resilience." I had never heard the term before, but it stuck with me. She explained how my experiences, no matter how painful, had built strength inside me that others could not see. She showed me what it meant to be a kind and compassionate human being. For the first time, I felt like I could do more than just survive—I could *thrive*.

That year, Ms. Johnstone's support became a lifeline. She didn't just teach me how to write essays; she helped me see that I was worthy of success. Her encouragement kept me going, even when the school system seemed set on pushing me out. My attendance record was a disaster—I had over seventy cuts, which put me at risk of being expelled. The school had a Student Attendance Review Board (SARB-3) meeting to decide my fate.

My parents weren't there to advocate for me, but Ms. Johnstone and the school psychologist, Ms. Dodd, stood up for me. Ms. Dodd had been working with me for a while, trying to understand my situation. During the meeting, she told the administrators that I wasn't just skipping school—I was homeless. She explained that my truancy wasn't defiance, but a reflection of the obstacles I faced daily.

Ms. Dodd didn't stop there. She came prepared with progress reports from my teachers, showing that I was capable and that my academic performance improved when I attended. I had even passed the California High School Exit Exam

(CHSEE) in ninth grade, a test that many of my peers were still struggling with.

Ms. Dodd also suggested emancipation as a solution. At eighteen, I could become my own legal guardian, allowing me to make decisions for myself without relying on my parents. With this newfound freedom, I was able to stay in school and graduate on time.

By the end of the year, I had caught up with my classmates and graduated with a 2.9 GPA. It wasn't perfect, but it was mine. After years of struggling, I had finally made it.

I often think about how different things could have been if I hadn't had people like Ms. Johnstone, Mr. Cuellar, and Ms. Dodd in my life. Healthy relationships, especially in a nurturing environment, are essential for growth. Without them, I might have become another statistic—another young Latino male lost to the streets or the prison system.

My friends and I grew up in trauma, and we didn't realize how much it shaped us. We didn't know how to deal with our pain, so we did what we were taught—numb it, hide it, or let it explode in destructive ways. Some of us made mistakes we couldn't come back from, like my friend Tox, who ended up in prison for the rest of his life.

The lessons I learned during my senior year stuck with me. I realized that being true to myself—my *authentic* self—was the only way forward. The system might try to push you down, but you have to rise above it. Don't let the game play you; learn how to play it.

"Your best is going to change from moment to moment; it will be different when you are healthy as opposed to sick. Under any circumstance, simply do your best, and you will avoid self-judgment, self-abuse, and regret."

—Don Miguel Ruiz, The Four Agreements

Reflection/Practice:

The power of a positive connection with a teacher or mentor can change the course of a life. For me, it was the "Big Three"— Mr. Cuellar, Ms. Johnstone, and Ms. Dodd—who saw through my pain and gave me the tools to believe in myself. They didn't just teach me history or English; they taught me how to be resilient and gave me the hope I needed to survive.

When someone truly sees you for who you are, it changes everything. They break the cycle of negativity and show you that you are worth something. I am living proof of that. Their compassion, patience, and belief in me gave me the strength to graduate and see beyond the obstacles I faced.

As I moved forward, I carried with me the lessons of resilience, kindness, and authenticity. I learned to embrace my strengths and acknowledge my weaknesses, but most importantly, I learned that it's okay to ask for help. It's okay to be vulnerable.

Takeaways:
- Never underestimate the impact of a kind word or gesture. It can change someone's life.
- Be true to yourself, even when the world tries to push you down.
- Build positive, healthy relationships with people who see you for who you truly are.
- Trust that your past does not define your future—you have the power to change your story.

CHAPTER 16:

THE HUSTLER'S MASK

After high school, I was still living a crazy and wild lifestyle. By the time I was eighteen, life had exhausted me, and I was unsure what to expect from life after high school. Senior year had become my only place of solace, and now, without it, I was losing the comfort I had recently learned to accept from the Big Three. It felt like losing family all over again. This time, however, there were no hard feelings, just the realization that I had to move forward. Yet, I was still grappling with the insecurities and anger that had plagued me as a boy, now manifesting in my young adult life.

Without positive mentors or anyone showing me my worth, I began seeking it elsewhere. The streets became my guide, and I imposed power on myself by not letting my emotions show. I convinced myself that I couldn't disappoint my former teachers. But in reality, I still needed to survive, and that survival led me to hustle full-time.

I earned a reputation as a leader on the streets, something that, in my mind, made me strong. I believed I had to maintain that image to keep respect. The independence I now had after high school was overwhelming. I had the freedom I had craved, but it was more than I knew what to do with. My teenage years had been tragic, and adulthood seemed just as stressful. The arrogance I had built as a shield only grew stronger, and hustling became my identity.

I didn't recognize pain anymore; I was masking it, living recklessly. The drive to make money, to buy the life I never had, consumed me. I feared failure more than anything because I had nothing to fall back on. I was entirely dependent on myself, and deep down, I longed for someone to hold me, to tell me everything would be okay. But where I came from, wishes didn't come true.

I became a hustler—one who supplied all sides of town. My life revolved around staying up all night and day to keep my hustle going. I didn't realize then that being around drugs constantly would eventually lead me to use them. At first, it didn't make me feel good, but over time, it numbed the loneliness. Soon, I didn't recognize the person I had become. I thought money, clothes, and material things would fill the void, but all it did was fuel the ego I was building.

Back in the '90s, everyone wanted to "be like Mike," and I had handles on the court. But I could never afford Jordans until I started hustling. Materialism got into my head. While I was still homeless and poor by most standards, hustling took me to places I had never been. As much as those spaces made me feel accepted, I had forgotten the wisdom my grandparents taught me. My ego had taken over, and I lost touch with who I truly was.

We often make decisions not in our best interest, driven by an ego that blinds us to our true self. I was hustling to survive, or so I told myself, but really, I was masking pain, insecurities, and the feeling of being lost. I lived through this inflated ego, feeling invincible, but in reality, I was just stuck in the fog of survival.

At this stage of life, I had no guidance, and the homies and I were simply trying to make it through the life we were handed. It felt like I had fallen from a second-story building after high school, unable to find my way. I needed to change my situation, but nothing else felt worth it. Hustling seemed like the only option.

One of the verses we created during a studio session at David's house back in 2005 captures my mindset at the time:

Moving bags of weight, money, guns, clothes, real estate,
Destin for a mill you can't interrupt fate,
Range rover on fifty acres plus the house on the lake,
Keep a good business, as well as dodge the fake,
Rats getting swallowed, devoured by us venomous snakes,
Hold down the fort regardless of what it takes,
Fuck a piece; give me the whole cake,
Plus a bulletproof and two nickel plates,
Fuck it, I'll get it done with one thirty-eight,
No shells for conviction, call it the great escape,
On top of the game, we call that checkmate,
Always ready for battle so we rock that war paint,
Started off as saints, got introduced to the game so now we ain't,
You want to get a sack off me but you caint,
So, stand back and witness the experience because you are about to faint.

This verse represents the hunger for survival, the desperation to escape poverty. Hustling gave me the money I needed to provide for myself, but it came at a cost. My ego grew, and so did my disconnect from who I really was.

The more I hustled, the more I tried to bury the pain and mask the suffering. The ego was a cover for the shame I carried. Once, someone crossed out my name on a wall—a form of disrespect in the streets. In a rage, I confronted and slapped the guy in front of everyone, letting my anger take over. I thought this would cement my reputation, but looking back, I realize it was just the ego reacting to shame and insecurity.

"The greatness of a man is not how much wealth he acquires, but in his integrity and his ability to affect those around him positively."

—Damian Marley

The more I hustled, the more I tried to bury the pain and mask the suffering. The ego was a cover for the shame I carried. Once, someone crossed out my name on a wall—a form of disrespect in the streets. In a rage, I confronted and slapped the guy in front of everyone, letting my anger take over. I thought this would cement my reputation, but looking back, I realize it was just the ego reacting to shame and insecurity.

As I matured, I began to understand how masking pain and building an ego only prolonged the suffering. I've spent a lot of time reflecting on how people, including myself, experience grief, how it impacts our lives, and how transformation begins when we address that suffering head-on. For those who don't address their pain, addiction, impulsive decisions, and harmful habits take root.

Many of us live unaware of how our suffering influences our actions. We fall into patterns that hurt us and the people around us. But the moment we become conscious of our pain, we can begin the healing process.

Ego often creates a false sense of identity, especially for those of us who grow up in environments that don't nurture our true selves. Society pushes us to believe we aren't good enough, leading to the creation of various masks to protect ourselves. But when we choose to lead with love, we start to dismantle the ego and open the door to healing.

Healing doesn't come easy, especially when we've been told to suppress our feelings. I was raised in a family that told me not to cry, to "man up." For years, I lived that way—until I realized that opening up and embracing vulnerability was the key to my growth. When I let go of my ego, I began to feel emotions I had long buried, and with that, came healing.

Now, think about your own journey. What masks are you wearing to hide your pain? Are you willing to confront those masks and let love lead the way to healing? Consider what your life would look like if money and ego weren't the focus. Who would you become if you let go of the hustle and embraced your authentic self? Write it down. Draw it out. Hang it where you can see it daily. Let this guide you to becoming who you were always meant to be.

The ability to see the bigger picture—beyond material success and the ego-driven desires—has helped me rid myself of the need to constantly prove my worth through money, status, or external validation. As I reflect on this journey, I realize how the hustle, while it seemed like my only option at the time, was just a way to mask deeper pain. The pursuit of material success made me believe that's where my value lay, but in reality, it only distanced me further from my true self.

I still battle my ego every day, but now, I am aware of it. I know that money and material success don't define me. What matters is staying true to myself, lifting others up, and finding purpose beyond wealth. This awareness has allowed me to build relationships and create work rooted in compassion, not competition or fear. It's taught me that real success comes from being able to positively affect others, to foster healing in myself and my community, and to leave a legacy of authenticity, love, and purpose.

When we rid ourselves of the masks and the ego, we open the door to true connection, growth, and fulfillment. And that, I believe, is the path to real success—one that transforms pain into power, suffering into wisdom, and fear into love.

CHAPTER 17:

UNCONDITIONAL LOVE

Being homeless, I was too busy trying to survive day by day, hiding my reality from those who would soon become the most valuable people in my life. I was terrified of people discovering my real situation. Dating girls or having a girlfriend threatened my ego because I didn't know how to value myself, much less someone else, at this time in my life.

Before my senior year, I had never been able to participate in the high school scene. I watched as my friends went to dances, football games, and basketball events. It always seemed so fun, and I longed to be a part of it, but my circumstances never allowed it. I convinced myself there was no place for me in these spaces because I couldn't afford to be in them. I became an expert at hiding behind that truth and protecting myself by keeping others at a distance.

When I met Marissa, everything changed. I first met her back in the sixth grade when she stepped off the bus while I was living at the Tangerine Hill Apartments. I had this purple-and-black bike and did my best to impress her when I saw her with her friends. We quickly went separate ways after middle school.

Reconnecting with her in high school was like a breath of fresh air. She transformed some of my suffering into happiness and hope. With her, I felt safe in a way I hadn't for a long time because I could be honest. But being with a girl like Marissa was hard while I was still homeless, selling drugs, and hiding much of my life. She knew I smoked weed, and while I kept the harder stuff hidden, she never judged me.

Marissa always gave me the gift of seeing life from a positive angle. She believed in me, and without her support, I don't know if I would have graduated or stayed in school. She was everything I had dreamed of—kind, funny, smart, and beautiful. She made my heart beat differently.

She came from a more privileged upbringing, with involvement in student government and cheerleading. I'd talk to her about oppression, social injustice, and racism from my perspective. She gave me strength when I felt weak and helped me with homework. Even though her mom wasn't a fan of me at first, she showed me compassion by cooking for us while we studied.

Her love and support created an environment where I could finally breathe. She made me believe I had a place in life. With her encouragement, I started building new habits and realized I could use my street smarts for a better life. Despite my struggles, for the first time since childhood, I began to feel that maybe I could be happy and that I could be loved.

At first, I tried to win her over with material things, thinking money was the answer. But Marissa didn't care about any of that. She only wanted my time, my attention, and my kindness. It wasn't until I was with her that I understood what unconditional love really was. Marissa showed me that love isn't something you can buy—it's earned through vulnerability, trust, and time.

"No one is born hating another person because of the color of his skin, background, or religion. People learn to hate, and if they learn to hate, they can be taught to love, for love comes more naturally to the human heart than its opposite."

—Nelson Mandela

Marissa's love and patience helped me realize that my ego was just a mask, something I wore to protect myself from pain. She showed me that being authentic was more powerful than any front I could put on. Her belief in me sparked something deep inside that made me want to be a better man. But giving her the love she deserved wasn't easy because I was still wrestling with so much from my past.

As men, we need to learn how sacred women are—whether they are partners, sisters, mothers, or even strangers. Without that nurturing energy, we might try to fill the void in unhealthy ways. It's a lie that showing love or emotions makes us weak. The real strength is being able to love, to express vulnerability, and to honor women for who they are.

The love I learned from Marissa changed me. It allowed me to feel emotions I hadn't felt in years and shed the ego I had built as a defense. Her love taught me that true power doesn't come from dominating others or building walls. It comes from being able to love and be loved, from understanding our pain and healing it, and from discovering our authentic selves.

Through her, I saw what real love looked like, and it set me on a journey that forever changed how I saw myself and the world. I now know that love isn't about what you can give someone materially—it's about who you are and how you show up for those you care about.

Unconditional love is the most powerful force on this earth, and when we experience it, it can change us in ways we never imagined.

But here's the truth: I didn't always know what love was. Growing up without the security of love or a safe home, I had no model to follow. Without love, life feels like survival. I spent years masking pain, letting my ego take control, and pretending I didn't need anyone. I thought I could hustle my way to happiness, that success was measured by money and status. But all of that was a cover for the loneliness I was too afraid to face.

Without love, we push people away. We sabotage relationships and miss out on real connection. It's not that we don't want love—we just don't know how to receive it. Love feels too risky, too vulnerable.

Marissa's patience showed me the truth. Real love doesn't demand anything from you. It doesn't ask you to be perfect or have all the answers. It simply asks you to be present, to show up as you are, and to trust that you are enough. That kind of love transforms.

Finding real love changes everything. It softens you, opens you up, and makes you realize you are worthy of being cared for. It teaches you that you don't need to hustle for validation. Love shows you that you are already enough.

I still battle my ego every day, but now, I am aware of it. I know that money and material success don't define me. What matters is staying true to myself, lifting others up, and finding purpose beyond wealth. What matters is love—because, in the end, love is what allows us to truly see each other and ourselves.

CHAPTER 18:

SOMETHING TO CONTRIBUTE

At this time, my living situation was still unstable. I needed to make money, so I continued hustling on the side until I could find a solid place to live. I dreamed of having a house and a stable job, but with no family support or trust fund waiting for me, it felt like an impossible goal. Though I made money, it wasn't legit. I remained homeless for several years after high school, spending money on drugs and just trying to survive. By the time I turned nineteen, I didn't even have a car. I had to pay people for rides or trade what little I had for favors. Sometimes, I would get robbed while staying at different people's houses, but that was the price of living from place to place.

As Marissa and I grew closer, she became the anchor in my life. She'd drive my friends and me to Reedley College, making sure we got to class on time. For the first time, I felt like I could become a productive member of society because of her belief in me. It felt like I had someone worth loving, someone who saw the good in me.

These were some of the better years of my life. Most kids my age were expected to go to college, but for many of us, the idea of a four-year university wasn't an option due to financial constraints. Reedley College was the best place we could afford, so we made it work. Marissa, always the diligent student, was a role model. Her discipline rubbed off on us, and we all began to take school seriously. For the first time since freshman year, all the homies were in school together—no one suspended, no one kicked out. We were living the dream, spending time together and focusing on something positive.

One night, my cousin J.R. visited me. After seeing where I was living, he told me I couldn't stay there anymore. The place wasn't safe for me, and he insisted I move in with him in Reedley. His timing was a blessing, especially with my newfound focus on school. I had just registered at Reedley College, and living with my cousin made everything easier. I had a safe place to stay, close to school, and I was reunited with family.

But life has a way of throwing curveballs. One night, while trying to get a sack of weed for a homie's birthday, things took a turn. We got pulled over for expired tags, and before I knew it, the cops were searching the car. Panic hit, and my instincts took over. I ran. I remember hiding out for hours, waiting for the sirens and cop lights to disappear. Eventually, I made it back to my cousin's apartment, where Marissa was waiting for me, concerned and scared. I thought I had gotten away, that life could go back to normal. I had a new job as a cashier at Rite-Aid, and with Marissa pregnant, I wanted to stay legit.

But the next day, the cops came looking for me at work. I was arrested. Sitting in the back of the cop car, I remember the officer's words, telling me that people like me would never amount to anything. Those words burned deep. As I got booked into county jail, I made my one phone call to Marissa. With the help of my cousin and his girlfriend, they bailed me out. I was relieved to be out, but I knew court was looming. I had saved up money in an old coat over the years, never trusting banks. I used that money to pay my cousin back and prepare for what was coming.

That night, I learned some hard lessons. I lost one of my closest friends, and I realized not everyone follows the same code. Trust was a hard thing to come by. I would soon learn that David was the only one who truly had my back.

"The highest form of knowledge is empathy, for it requires us to suspend our egos and live in another's world."

—Plato

_____

At this stage of my life, I wanted to do better, but I had developed so many habits over the years of surviving on my own. By nineteen, I was good at making money illegally, and the thought of change felt daunting. But being with Marissa helped me see the world differently. I knew I had to change my lifestyle if I wanted us to stay together. Jail opened my eyes. I saw that hustling could put me in prison for good, and I didn't want that. I began challenging myself to change.

I started playing basketball and football, anywhere I could find a game. I began reading more, writing poetry, and having dreams about a future outside the hood. I dreamed of getting a degree, finding a good job, and creating a loving family. For so long, I thought hustling was my only way out, but now, I was beginning to see a different path. Despite all the challenges, I believed that if I had survived being homeless, getting kicked out of school, and battling addiction, I could do anything.

Becoming aware of my existence, of my potential, was liberating. I realized that at any moment, we have the power to step into a mindset that can create a positive future. Change starts with how we see ourselves and how we speak to ourselves. Learning to love myself was like building muscle—it took time, practice, and effort and it was hard because it did not come naturally.

For those of us who grew up in places like Poverty 4x, self-compassion is something we rarely learn. We're often out of shape when it comes to loving ourselves, and we need to strengthen that skill just like we would our bodies. Later, in the chapter titled "The Buddha," I'll dive deeper into self-compassion and how it can transform not only your life but the lives of others.

CHAPTER 19:

FATHERHOOD AND COMMUNITY COLLEGE

At 9:02 a.m. on April 18, 2006, I became a father at just twenty years old. I was scared out of my mind. I didn't know if I could be a good dad. At the time, I was hustling, carrying trauma that I believed was visible to everyone. Hustling was how I kept paying for school, but I wasn't thriving in college. Marissa, on the other hand, showed no fear, though I knew she was scared after our son was born. She felt ashamed, afraid of disappointing people, and convinced she was letting her mom down. She hid her pregnancy for the first seven months because she had no one to turn to—not even me. In those moments, all we had was each other, and I believed hustling was the fastest way to build a home for our family.

One day, Marissa's stepdad came home early. He was someone Marissa could talk to most of the time. We were sitting on the couch when he walked over and calmly asked, "So, are you pregnant, Mija?" Marissa's eyes swelled with tears as she nodded. He hugged her and told her it would be okay, but now we'd have to tell her mom. When her mom came home, she could barely speak—she was upset and didn't accept the news easily. Marissa's growing belly could no longer be hidden. Despite our struggles, Marissa made sure I was with my son every moment of his life. She saw how much love I had for our boy and never thought about keeping him from me. But there was a sadness within her. Her relationship with her mom weighed heavy on her, but amidst the tension, one of her aunts invited us to stay with her, giving us a roof over our heads until we could find a place of our own.

At the time, I was attending Reedley Community College and on probation. My life was a constant balancing act. I had to go to school five days a week, get drug tested twice a week, and attend Narcotics Anonymous and Alcoholics Anonymous (NA/AA) meetings twice a week—often driving over thirty miles to get there. I was doing my best to juggle everything, but it was overwhelming, and I had no one to talk to about it. Life was getting harder, and one day, I made a bad choice. After nine months of being clean, I failed a drug test and was locked up for twenty-one days.

Before my son was born, I had applied for Section Eight, low-income housing. A few months after he was born, I was granted a stipend. That made me eligible for cash aid and food stamps, and soon after, we moved into an apartment in Parlier. I felt grateful but conflicted. Being on Section Eight felt like I was repeating the same cycle I was born into—poverty, government assistance, and no real hope for a brighter future. As the father and a leader of my family, I couldn't allow myself to be consumed by hopelessness or the street mentality I'd grown up with. I didn't want my son to feel the same lack of belonging I had felt as a child. I was lost, overwhelmed by fatherhood, and burdened with the responsibility I wasn't prepared for.

When I got out of jail, I remember seeing my son crawling around on the floor. I looked at Marissa, and a flood of memories from my childhood hit me. I saw flashes of my parents' fights, the false promises, the absence of real moments with my dad. I thought of all the pain I experienced growing up and told myself that I wouldn't let my son go through the same thing. I wanted to give him the best, but I had no idea how because all I'd ever known was suffering. I saw in my son's eyes everything I had been running from in my past. I wanted to be the father I wished I had, to break the cycle of trauma and create a different life for him. That moment marked a turning point for me, even though I didn't have all the answers.

I reflected on what it meant to be a parent. Becoming a father wasn't just about survival anymore—it was about creating something new. I wanted to give him the happiness I never had. But I was stuck in survival mode—trying to provide for my family, go to school, hold down a job, and figure out how to be a man.

I couldn't allow myself to be swallowed by the hopelessness or the street mentality that told me I'd never succeed or be loved. But at twenty, I was still consumed by my ego and old habits. I fell back into hustling hard, meeting new people, and taking bigger risks. I was on probation, and the fear of getting caught again was always with me. I kept hustling because it was all I knew, but I kept Marissa and our son far from it. I didn't know what else to do. I had no one to guide me, no roadmap for young parents like us.

Yet, somehow, I was blessed. While I was locked up, I had built relationships with three professors at Reedley Community College—Mrs. McCain, Ms. Bartram, and Mr. Rodriquez. They showed me compassion I hadn't seen from many others. With Marissa's help, they gathered all my missed assignments so I could pass my classes. These professors believed in me when I struggled to believe in myself. Looking back, I often wonder if I'd have made it through school without them. They showed me my worth when I felt worthless, and I'll forever be grateful.

"Instead of buying your children all the things you never had, you should teach them all the things you were never taught. Material wears out, but knowledge stays."

—Bruce Lee

———————

I realized that the most valuable things I could give my children weren't material. I wanted to teach them what I hadn't been taught—to pass down lessons about love, resilience, and how to build a life that didn't just survive but thrive. These were the things I wished I had learned early in life.

No matter where you are, you must keep trying. Push yourself to do something positive with your life. Mistakes are lessons. When we take time to reflect, we become aware of how we can do better. You may not feel like you deserve good things—many of us are told that—but that's a lie. Finding happiness and reaching your potential is your birthright. It's hard to push past the pain and negative thoughts, but if you don't try, you'll never know what's possible. My abuelo once taught me to seguir adelante—keep moving forward. There were times when I fell, but I always got up. Now I had a reason bigger than myself to keep going: my son.

I was beyond blessed to have my son, and for him to have a mother who poured every ounce of love into raising him. Marissa stayed strong through it all. She kept us connected as a family, no matter how hard things got. The bond between a mother and child is a beautiful thing, and I could finally feel it. We weren't rich by any means. Marissa stayed home to care for our son and helped her family, and I was doing whatever I could to provide. I invited my brothers over as often as I could. We played football, basketball, video games—anything that brought joy and laughter into our lives. I was building the environment I'd wished we had as kids. My brothers were proud uncles, and I was proud to have a family filled with love, even if it wasn't perfect.

Marissa's steady presence was a rock during this time. She helped me see that being a father meant more than just providing. It meant creating a home filled with love and showing up every day. Her strength was a reminder of the family we were building together, and she never let me lose sight of that.

My abuelo's spirit, my son, Santana, and later my daughter, Leilah Rose, have been my guiding lights. Their love heals me every day. If we don't heal the trauma we've lived through, it stays with us, lingering in our bodies and passing on to the next generation. Healing isn't just for us—it's for our children and their children. By doing the work to heal, we become better husbands, fathers, and men. We can show up for our women and ensure that the next generation thrives, rather than just survives.

My son's existence shifted my entire universe, but the birth of my daughter, Leilah Rose, took that transformation to another level. Becoming a father for the second time made me realize that my responsibility was no longer just about surviving. It was about creating a life where both of my children could thrive— free from the cycles of pain and struggle I had known my entire life.

Leilah's arrival sparked something profound inside me. I wasn't just raising children; I was nurturing souls that deserved a future far removed from the hardships I had faced. Her presence made me recognize that I could no longer live the life of hustling and running—there was no room for half-measures anymore. I had to be all in, for her and for Santana. I had to break the cycle once and for all, without any repeats of the past.

Looking into Leilah's eyes, I felt the weight of my choices. This time, it wasn't just about making it through the day or hustling to survive. It was about building a future, a real future where both my children could thrive—free from the pain I had carried for so long. I knew that if I didn't break the cycle now, it would pass to them, and that was something I couldn't let happen. At that moment, I realized I had to leave behind the old ways for good. No more half-stepping, no more excuses. My children deserved better, and I was going to give them the life

and love they deserved, no matter the cost. I would fight for
them, just as I had fought for myself to survive but this time do
it in a legal and legit way.

CHAPTER 20:

DAVID

Once I was off probation, I started spending time with people I could genuinely trust. As my son grew, David and I began to hang out more often. During this time, we started to monopolize as hustlers in the places we were living. Finding a legit job was part of the plan for Santana's future, but at that moment, we were living a different path. Our gospel was the Wu-Tang Clan. We lived out their principles and philosophies, believing we were on a quest to heal humanity with what we all loved in common—weed. We both believed strongly in it because it helped us cope with our trauma, and we thought it could help others do the same. At least, that's what we told ourselves.

David had moved closer to town, making it easier for us to hang out and make music. I started going to the studio more often with him. I had introduced David to a homie I met in my criminology class who also made beats. Coincidentally, his grandma's house was just down the street from David's new place.

One night, David threw a party to celebrate his birthday and invited everyone from the block. My cousins were there, too, and I remember David freestyling on top of the table in the homie's grandma's backyard. We hadn't been together like that in a while, and it felt like we were kids again. I didn't want the night to end—it was pure joy. For me, friends were the family I got to choose, and David was my brother in every sense of the word. But like life always does, things shifted quickly. David, the romantic he was, left the party early to make his girl happy. I never imagined that would be the last time I'd see him or feel his presence in this world.

That night, I went back to Marissa's mom's house, feeling so happy. I had my best friend, my family, and my girl in the same place. Life felt good. But the next day, July 1, 2007, everything changed. I got a call at 4:00 a.m. from Manz, a younger homie David had introduced me to. He called to tell me that David was dead. At first, I thought he was lying. This was David—Ferm— my soul brother, the one person who truly accepted me for who I was. I couldn't believe what he was saying.

David "Ferm" Vera was killed on the outskirts of Sanger on July 1, 2007. The chaos that led to his murder started around 2:30 a.m. He had been shot twice in the chest while trying to direct traffic after someone else had been shot at the party.

David was doing what he always did—trying to help. It felt like the world had ripped my soul away. Breathing became hard. It was as if the light had been sucked out of the hood, the way it felt when we heard that 2Pac had been shot. David was too strong, too full of life, to be gone.

The pain hit the entire community hard. Everyone was in shock. The shooter, and the person responsible for David's death, fled the scene. It took ten years of persistence from the Vera family, but eventually, those responsible were brought in, charged, and found guilty of murder.

David and I are pictured in the high school yearbook, voted "best buds" by our classmates. It was an easy choice, Marissa said. Our peers saw something in us that we didn't always recognize in ourselves. Growing up in the streets, David and I fit together like pieces of a puzzle. In school, we were labeled leaders of our clique. The high school administration even told us that if there was ever graffiti on our corner, we'd be the first to be blamed. People recognized the influence we had, even when we didn't.

When David was killed, it felt like a piece of my soul was taken with him. His death sparked an anger and pain inside me that I didn't know how to process. It made me question the life I was living and where it was leading. People I had once considered David's brothers, people I would've died for, started doing things that were disrespectful to his name and possessions. This was when the harsh realities of trauma began to show me a new truth—one that swallowed me alive.

David's death taught me hard lessons about authenticity and values. It showed me how quickly friends could turn to enemies when it served them. I didn't understand suffering then as I do now. I didn't realize that these people were suffering too, acting out in foolish ways to cope with their own pain. We were all expressing our pain differently, but without that understanding, I would have stayed angry and disappointed in them.

I started to feel the same sense of displacement that I had felt as a child, like I didn't belong anywhere. Seeing the way people acted after David's death, I knew I had to refocus my life. I chose to concentrate on school, my son, and my family. But even as I did that, the loneliness set in. I felt like I had lost my way without David. His death, and the earlier loss of my friend Ray Ruiz Jr., who had been stabbed to death, took a toll on my mind, body, and soul.

The grief overwhelmed me. To cope, I returned to destructive behaviors—hustling, working hard, and burying myself in distractions. I thought I was resilient because I was functioning, making money, going to school. But deep down, I was broken. I didn't know how to deal with grief. My emotions were numb. The saturation of pain in my life was so great that I convinced myself it was normal. I kept moving forward, pretending the pain wasn't there.

David's death set me back. I didn't have the wisdom or courage to find new ways to live, so I reverted to old habits. I isolated myself from friends who had turned to drugs and foolish behavior. I viewed the world as fake, and I felt mad at everything. My focus shifted to making money, attending school, and getting out of the hood. But the emptiness David left behind never fully went away.

One day, my EOPS counselor asked if I wanted to transfer to a university. It was like David had returned from the dead, pushing me forward once again. I had never dreamed of going to a university, but something inside me told me I could get ahead if I kept going. I was scared, though. I was twenty-one, living on Section Eight, fresh out of jail, with no high school diploma, no family support, and nothing but my hustle and school. It didn't feel like I had what it took to succeed.

David had always been there to guide me, but now I was alone. I didn't fully realize how much he meant to me until he was gone. He had always pushed me to be better—in everything from sports to being a man. It took years to cope with the void his death left. I remember breaking down to Marissa, finally letting myself feel the loss, the heartache, and the confusion. I cried so hard, the pain hit me deep in my stomach. That's when it fully sank in that David was really gone.

"Tell your friend that in his death, a part of you dies and goes with him. Wherever he goes, you also go. He will not be alone."

—Jiddu Krishnamurti

———————

I still dream about calling his house sometimes. I remember his phone number by heart. In my dreams, I dial it, hoping he'll answer. But when I wake up, I realize it was just a dream. David's death taught me that grieving isn't something you just get over—it's a long journey, a part of you now. Every day, I honor his name and what he stood for by pushing myself to be the best I can be. I make sure his legacy lives on. David taught me to stand firm in everything I do and to carry pride, honor, and respect for myself and others because that is how he carried himself and what made him who he was.

CHAPTER 21:

STREET ACADEMIC

"The beautiful thing about learning is that no one can take it away from you."

—B.B. King

Attending California State University at Fresno (Fresno State) was the biggest challenge I had ever faced. For someone who had only completed one full year of high school, stepping into this massive world was overwhelming. I didn't know how I would navigate this academic life. At first, I was a business major, but something felt off. I wanted to do more—something rooted in humanity, something that allowed me to take my lived experiences and turn them into something meaningful. I wanted to inspire systems, policies, and people. But before I could get into the social work program, I had to face the harsh reality: my GPA wasn't high enough.

I didn't let that stop me. I set up a meeting with Dr. John Franz, the department chair, and he took a chance on me. He let me into the program on probation. Dr. Franz was this tall, white man, but his compassion and brilliance radiated. It was like he took it personally when he told me that I wouldn't fail. He taught me that I already knew a lot about social work through my tragic life experiences, but I needed to embark on a healing journey before I could truly serve others.

Connecting with professors like Dr. Franz, who offered me not just knowledge but compassion and belief, inspired me to join clubs and social work events. That's when I started my quest to give back. I found myself in office hours, having deep conversations about empirical theories, and using those theories to understand my shame, insecurities, and resilience. I started making sense of my past—childhood trauma, cultural disconnection, and the weight of being a young parent while trying to fit into this academic world.

I struggled with imposter syndrome constantly. I felt like an outsider in higher education, lost without mentors or guidance. I wanted to give up so many times, but I couldn't. Role models like Dr. Anne Petrovich, Virginia Hernandez, Chris Cole, Margaret Jackson, Sharon Chun-Wetterau, Wanda MacIntosh, David Plassman, and Dr. Martha Vungkhanching appeared in my life like my personal Avengers. Each one brought their own brand of wisdom, rooted in non-judgment and compassion. They encouraged me to be myself and to lead with my raw, insightful experience. It wasn't the curriculum that changed my life—it was their humanity.

As I dove deeper into my studies, I learned about neuroscience and the psychology of why people did what they did. It fascinated me. I started reading Krishnamurti, Alan Watts, Deepak Chopra, Thich Nhat Hanh, Don Miguel Ruiz, and Paulo Freire. The world began to make sense from where I stood. Books like *The 48 Laws of Power* by Robert Greene and studies on trauma opened my eyes to the roots of suffering. I started to see ways I could liberate myself, but the responsibilities of fatherhood, paying for school, rent, and everything else still weighed heavy on me.

Years of hustling had made me good at organizing my life, making money, and avoiding danger. But it also created a duality in me. I wanted to be successful in school, but I still had to find time to hustle to support my family. The balance was hard. My only way out was to finish my master's degree without falling back into the streets. I applied what I was learning in social work to myself—healing my own trauma as I helped others.

One of the things that kept me engaged in the program was conducting ethnographic interviews in spaces where gangs operated. My past knowledge of gang life gave me unique access. I was able to explore why people joined gangs and how they survived. One assignment involved creating a community asset map of Sanger, where I saw redlining firsthand. Liquor stores lined one side of town while the other side thrived. I started to realize that much of our suffering—poverty, racism, discrimination—wasn't accidental. It was by design.

After graduating with my bachelor's degree in 2010, I applied for a master's program. I was excited but terrified. One faculty member even told me I shouldn't be in the program because of my past—because I had been homeless, jailed, and battled addiction. I couldn't believe what I was hearing after coming so far. But I didn't let it stop me. I knew my worth. I understood how vital integrity and relationships with professors were, especially when dealing with oppression and marginalization. I advocated for myself, and I proved that faculty member wrong. Not only did I make it into the program, but I also worked in schools, despite being told I never could.

That experience made me think about how many students, especially those of color or living in poverty, face gatekeepers who hold them back. It reminded me how important it is to advocate for yourself and for others.

Once I was in the field, I was determined to make a change. I couldn't believe someone like me—someone who grew up homeless, went to Juvenile Hall, was addicted to drugs, and hustled to survive—could earn a master's degree. It felt unreal, but I was living proof that it was possible. Hip-hop had raised me, and the injustices I saw in the world fueled my fire. But that also caused friction with some of my professors who couldn't relate to the world I came from.

Most of the professors were intelligent, but they were disconnected from the realities of the community. What they taught us wasn't always helpful in practice. I often challenged them in class, bringing the raw truth from my experiences. Some didn't like that. They tried to put me back in a box, but I couldn't let them. My experiences showed me that people from the hood weren't broken. They weren't flawed. They were survivors, and I had to find a way to help others see that.

After the first year of my master's program, I felt happier. I was more engaged in my education and appreciative of what I had. Hustling had made me driven by money and ego, but now I was learning about suffering—my own and the world's. I started to see the small ways I could make a difference and reduce suffering. This transformation deepened my relationship with Marissa and allowed me to peel back layers of trauma that had held me back my whole life.

During the summer, I read an article on neuroplasticity. It blew my mind. My whole life, I thought my brain was fixed—born into trauma and brokenness. But I learned that my brain could change. It could grow. This idea of neuroplasticity was life-changing for me. I began devouring books like *The Art of War*, *The Prince* , *How to Win Friends and Influence People* , and biographies of Malcolm X, Huey P. Newton, and Che Guevara. These were the rebels and thinkers I had heard about in the lyrics of 2Pac, Wu-Tang Clan, and UGK.

As I became more studious, I wondered if social work was truly where I could help others who came from chaotic lives like mine. The theories I learned helped me understand my own brokenness. I infused techniques from Carl Rogers into my daily life, started journaling, and writing poetry. It became a way to document my pain, gratitude, and growth. I learned to speak my truth through writing, a practice David had always encouraged me to do.

By the end of my first two years in the master's program, I began to realize how much power I had over my own narrative. I found teachers who understood me, and I used my knowledge to create real change. I even landed my first job in the field—a part-time gig as a cultural broker for Fresno County, working with Child Protective Services to help them become more culturally sensitive.

"Sometimes, we have to promote ourselves. Just go out and be very active about trying to find an opportunity."

—Dolores Huerta

———————

I was finding my voice. I started visiting an Ethiopian store in Fresno and learning about Emperor Haile Selassie. The owners became friends, and I found joy in their music—Reggae artists like Sizzla and Capleton became part of my journey. Life started to feel like it was falling into place. My heart felt full again, and I realized that I could blend my street smarts with the academic knowledge I had gained.

After a lifetime of struggle, I finally found my place in the world. People had told me I wouldn't make it, but I proved them wrong. I began to heal from the abuse, neglect, and shame that had defined my life. I learned to forgive myself for the things I didn't understand when I was younger. The shame that had once held me back began to dissolve. I learned that I wasn't cursed—I had just been conditioned by a world that didn't know how to nurture people like me. And I was finally learning how to love myself and make sense of my trauma and behavior."

CHAPTER 22:

SAMMY

"Grief is love looking for a home."

—Susan David

When Sammy was killed, it shattered the illusion I had once held about the lifestyle I had celebrated. Hustling had seemed like a way out, a way to survive, but now it was clear that it had brought nothing but suffering. What I thought was power had turned into a curse, and the choices I made in my past began to haunt the future I was struggling to build. Sammy looked up to me—I was his big brother, his role model—and because of that, my brothers had followed in my footsteps, seeing the same easy access to drugs and notoriety that I had. I was ashamed that my past had shaped their choices. We learned to survive in the only way we knew how, especially with our mom on disability, struggling to provide. But I realized too late that the path I chose had devastating consequences.

Sammy's death taught me something I had been avoiding for years—that my hustle was a way of coping with my own suffering. I had been using it to mask the pain, to create a reputation, but now, as a father, I knew I never wanted my son to see me in that same light. This realization, combined with what I was learning in school, sparked a fierce determination in me. I wanted to help kids growing up like Sammy and me, to find a way to use my education to lessen their suffering if they ever became ready to open up and share their pain.

Sammy's death forced me to confront a deeper truth about resilience: being resilient doesn't mean you've healed. I was holding down my family, going to school, making money—on the surface, I was doing well. But underneath it all, I was barely processing my trauma. People would tell me I was strong, that I had survived so much, but inside, I felt like I was crumbling. I blamed myself for Sammy's choices, for the life he lived that led to his death. The same negative self-talk I'd fought my entire life came back stronger than ever. Once again, I felt flawed, as if I was the reason for his death.

When Sammy went missing, I held onto the pain, refusing to let myself truly feel it. I acted as if it didn't bother me, but I was angry—angry all the time. Then, when we finally learned Sammy had been killed, it was a blow unlike anything I had experienced. My son came home from kindergarten, and another child told him that his Uncle Sammy had been shot, that he had seen it on the news. The fact that my son learned about it this way broke me even more. But I was blessed to have compassionate people around me—his teacher, Mrs. McCallum, and the staff at the school were incredible. They protected my son from fear and confusion and supported us as we navigated the situation.

As I tried to process Sammy's death, I realized that I had no idea how to grieve. The pain was overwhelming, the worst I had ever experienced in my life. Sammy's birthday passed while he was missing—his birthday, just two days after mine and three days after Marissa's, was always a time we celebrated together. Now, that celebration turned into a reminder of everything I had lost.

When the trial began, we learned the horrific details of what had happened to him. Sammy had been shot several times with an AK-47, then buried in a ditch, as if his life meant nothing. The main suspect was caught with 20 pounds of marijuana while trying to cross into Utah. The trial dragged on for years, but in the end, justice was hollow. One man served five years for gun possession, and the other two who were involved were granted immunity. They never faced real consequences for taking my brother's life. The system allowed them to escape justice, and that only deepened the pain.

As I navigated this grief, I found myself growing closer to my mom. We had always been outcasts in some ways, but now we leaned on each other more than ever. She had always been okay with being labeled and misunderstood, but this time, we found a new bond. At the same time, my relationship with Marissa began to drift. She was pregnant with our daughter, Leilah Rose, throughout the time Sammy was missing, and I was too broken to be the father or partner I wanted to be. Sammy's death, combined with my inability to process the pain, made me feel like I was failing everyone—Marissa, my children, and myself.

Life is a parallel process . If you feed into suffering, you spread suffering. But if you transform it, you can radiate compassion and healing. That's a truth I slowly came to understand as I began to develop mindfulness practices and started reflecting more deeply on my emotions, trauma, and healing. Sitting still with my pain showed me something I had been running from my whole life: those who shot my brother were suffering too. This insight shifted something in me. I realized that holding onto hate would only create more suffering—for them, for me, for everyone. The system allowed them to escape punishment, but they would have to live with their choices for the rest of their lives. That was enough.

I learned that forgiveness—of others, and of myself—was the only path to liberation. For years, I had blamed myself. If only I had been there for Sammy more, if only I had given him better advice, if only I had been home the night he wanted to come over—maybe things would have turned out differently. But I had to let go of that. I wasn't perfect, but I did the best I could with what I knew at the time. And that had to be enough.

"Someone can intentionally send you emotional poison. And if you don't take it personally, it will not affect you."

—Don Miguel Ruiz

Sammy's death forced me to face my own grief in ways I hadn't with David's passing. I realized I had been in denial about David's death for years, refusing to feel the full weight of it. But with Sammy, the anger, the bargaining, the depression—they all hit hard. I spent so much time wondering what I could have done differently, blaming myself. But I finally came to understand that their deaths were not my fault.

Talking about Sammy with my daughter helped me heal. For years, I didn't know how to explain his death to her, but as I began to share memories of him, I found comfort in remembering the good times we had. That's when I started to truly heal. David and Sammy may be gone, but I can honor them by living a life that keeps their spirit alive.

Forgiveness doesn't come easy, but it's the only way to truly find peace. The men who killed my brother and my best friend were trapped in their own suffering, living in survival mode like so many of us do. Holding onto the pain and the hate only kept me stuck in that same cycle. But when I let go, I found a path to healing. Every time someone breaks free from that cycle of suffering, they open up new possibilities for future generations. That's what I've learned from losing David and Sammy. Healing isn't just about me—it's about breaking the chains of trauma for those who come after us.

CHAPTER 23:

FLIPPING THE SCRIPT

"Education does not change the world. Education changes people. People change the world."

—Paulo Freire

———————

Losing my brother, Sammy, and my friend, David, left me feeling lost, confused, angry, and hopeless all over again. These tragedies hit just as I was starting to feel like I was finding my way—balancing school, being a good father, and getting my life on track. David's death came when I was in community college and thought I was doing well. But his loss threw me into a tailspin. I didn't know how to grieve, and I didn't know who to turn to for help. The grief was like a wound I couldn't heal. There's a saying: "Hurt people hurt people." For years, I indulged in behaviors that made my ego feel alive, but in reality,

I was hurting myself and others. Losing my best friend and my youngest brother reignited all the unresolved pain from my childhood.

When Sammy died, shame hit me hard. I didn't know how to love or heal myself. His death brought back all the unresolved feelings from David's death and stirred up old anger from being alone and homeless as a kid. It felt like everything I'd been trying to bury was rising back to the surface, and this time, I didn't have my best friend or my brother to help me through it.

This is where I began to realize that forgiveness—of others and of myself—was the most liberating thing I could do. For years, I had carried the weight of guilt, thinking that if I had just done something differently, things wouldn't have turned out this way. But forgiveness released me from that self-imposed prison. It helped me see the bigger picture—why things happen the way they do, and what steps we need to take to break free from the cycles of suffering that trap so many of us.

As I sat with these thoughts, I began to realize the real change had to start within me. I needed to re-engineer how I navigated the world, how I responded to suffering—not just with survival, but with compassion. Compassion for others and, just as importantly, compassion for myself. When I stumbled, I had to learn to forgive myself while holding onto the discipline to keep growing. I had to rediscover the person I was before the world and its hardships had reshaped how I viewed myself and reality.

There were times in my life when I wasn't the nicest person. Being kind didn't come naturally to me, especially when I was dealing with people who caused more suffering for me and others. My ego, fueled by my insecurities, often took over. I carried so much hurt and hate inside me that I didn't know what to do with it. Growing up in a male-dominated family that operated on machismo and told me to never cry, I didn't learn how to talk about my emotions or face them with compassion. I was taught to "man up," to keep it all inside. Once I let go of that toxic myth, I began to feel my heart open in ways it never had before. I learned that the negative emotions I was holding onto were products of my suffering, and by transforming my mindset, I could also transform my reality.

Psychologist Susan David says that self-compassion is the antidote to shame, and learning to love myself—really love who I am—was the key to changing that inner dialogue. I began to walk in my truth, knowing that I had the strength of generations behind me, and this helped me let go of the shame. I started to speak my truth, even to those who didn't want to hear it, but always from a place of compassion. When I did something wrong in the past, it wasn't because I knew better; it was because I didn't. Now that I know better, I can do better, and that's the philosophy I live by today.

You know that little voice in your head that tells you you're not good enough? For me, that voice was loud, relentless, and cruel. It constantly told me I wasn't shit, that I was a failure. But over time, I learned how to quiet that voice. I began to remember the lessons my abuela and abuelo taught me, the stories they told me about where I came from. I felt a deep sense of guilt that I had lost my language, lost my connection to my roots. In my late twenties and early thirties, I started attending healing circles and men's retreats. Listening to other men be vulnerable and share their stories helped me realize I wasn't alone in my struggles.

One of the most profound moments for me came when another man shared advice on how to connect with my daughter. He told me to take her dancing, bring her flowers, and make time for her in ways I hadn't known how to before. I grew up around men like my father, and while it was easy for me to connect with my son, I didn't know how to be gentle, sensitive, or understanding with my daughter. This advice changed everything for me.

"Maybe the journey isn't so much about becoming anything. Maybe it's about unbecoming everything that isn't really you, so you can be who you were meant to be in the first place."

—Paulo Coelho

As I worked on flipping that negative inner voice, I began to ask myself: What would David or Sammy say to me right now? Their spirits were still with me, guiding me in a more positive direction. Even though they were gone, they helped me change how I spoke to myself. I started to show myself kindness, and as I did, I felt more love for others as well. The hate, pain, and judgment slowly faded away, replaced with a desire to help others avoid the suffering I had endured.

I honor Sammy and David's lives by telling their stories and connecting with students who are like we were. I try to help those who don't understand people like us, teaching them to approach with compassion instead of judgment. It's incredible how we can transform the worst experiences of our lives into gifts we share with others. Every time I think about David and Sammy, I'm reminded that I'm still here for a purpose.

Whenever I feel overwhelmed, I find a quiet place where no one can reach me for five or ten minutes. I sit with my back against the wall, my spine straight, and I breathe deeply. As I inhale, I fill my lungs completely. I count to four, hold the breath for four seconds, and then exhale slowly, imagining that with each breath, I am releasing the stress and tension inside me. Once I'm settled, I picture myself and my current struggles. I ask, what advice would Sammy or David give me right now?

How would they guide me out of this? After this reflection, I write down everything that comes to mind.

This practice is for me—no one else needs to understand it. But it helps me connect with the wisdom of those who loved me and see my problems from a different perspective. It allows me to become my own best friend, to love myself in ways I never learned as a child. We have to live with ourselves every day, and if we don't learn to like and care for ourselves, we're doomed to stay stuck in the same harmful cycles. Flipping the script on that inner voice is the key to creating the life we deserve, one rooted in love, compassion, and authenticity.

CHAPTER 24:

BUDDHA

"Be like water."

—*Paulo Freire*

———————

In 2018, I came across the Compassion Institute, developed in 2009 at Stanford University by Thupten Jinpa, Ph.D., and other founding faculty members. They offered classes on cultivating compassion, which intrigued me because it seemed like a different form of therapy, a path to healing from my lifetime of trauma. It felt like the treatment I had been seeking for years. My teacher during this journey was Erika Rosenberg, who provided a transformative experience, guiding me to rediscover my authentic self.

For years, I had been caught up in negative emotional patterns, convinced I could never truly be happy, compassionate, or even a good person. But through intentional practices like self-compassion, gratitude, forgiveness, and reexamining childhood myths about masculinity, I began to see the light. I started to understand my emotions, see how they shaped my behaviors, and recognize the patterns that kept me locked in suffering. Self-compassion became my anchor, allowing me to wish others well, forgive myself, and break free from the ego-driven narratives that had kept me stuck for so long.

When my brother Sammy went missing, my commitment to mindfulness faltered. His disappearance brought overwhelming pain, and I struggled to stay grounded. But through the Compassion Institute's teachings, I found a way back. I realized that compassion—both for myself and others—was not just a concept but a necessity. I began to recognize that I needed spiritual guidance to navigate this complex journey. In my culture, seeking help from a therapist had always been frowned upon, but as a social worker, I knew I had to find someone who could help me unlock this part of myself.

Around that time, I entered a mentorship program with Dr. Siri Sat Nam Singh. I learned to apply the principles of compassion cultivation to my own life. Dr. Gabor Maté's words rang true for me: "Trauma is not what happens to you, it's what happens inside you as a result of what happened to you." Those words resonated deeply because I was still carrying the trauma of my childhood, of losing my brother and my best friend, and I didn't know how to release it. Dr. Maté's insights about how trauma scars us—making us less flexible, more rigid, and more defended—gave me the tools to start healing those scars.

Through meditation and self-reflection, I learned to revisit my younger self—the boy who never received the compassion he needed—and offer him the love he had been denied. This process was painful, but it allowed me to rediscover who I had been before the world taught me to shut down. Slowly, I began to feel lighter, more free, and more connected to the joy I once knew.

"Compassion" comes from the Latin words "com," meaning together, and "passion," meaning to suffer. So compassion means "to suffer together."

In Lak'ech Ala K'in is the Mayan moral code that means "You are my other me. What I do unto you, I do unto myself." Ubuntu, an African philosophy often associated with Nelson Mandela, teaches that we are bound together in ways that are invisible to the eye and that we find ourselves by sharing ourselves with others. The Buddha taught that true compassion must include oneself. These teachings began to reshape how I interacted with the world. I could now see the common humanity in everyone and understood that my destructive behaviors had stemmed from suffering. But now, with compassion as my guide, I could transform those behaviors.

For much of my life, I lived with a false narrative about who I was and what I was capable of becoming. I was too ashamed to share my true self, afraid people would see me as weak or unstable because of my past. But as I grew in self-compassion,

I realized that by not sharing my story, I was denying others the opportunity to see how suffering can lead to wisdom and healing.

We live in a world where people are more disconnected than ever—suicide rates are at an all-time high, conflict leads to violence, and mental health issues are rampant. We've normalized working and schooling through this chaos, but the truth is, many of us are deeply unhappy. Self-compassion taught me that we cannot offer true compassion to others until we first cultivate it within ourselves.

When we are consumed by anger, fear, jealousy, or sadness, it's hard to extend compassion. We must step into our pain, not run from it. Naming our emotions is a powerful way to start releasing ourselves from their grip. As I learned to name my emotions, I found that they no longer controlled me. Instead of drowning in anger or sadness, I could observe those feelings, acknowledge them, and then release them. This practice helped me separate myself from the destructive emotions that had once dictated my life.

Learning to meditate with self-compassionate mindfulness has given me the space to understand how my emotions influence my behavior. I saw how much of my suffering was rooted in the past and how my unchecked trauma shaped the patterns of my life. Writing, sitting in solitude, and reflecting on my journey allowed me to confront the parts of myself that were still broken. If I was going to heal, I had to dedicate my life to compassion and release the pain that had been holding me back.

"If your compassion does not include yourself, it is incomplete."

—The Buddha

Self-compassion has taught me to give my love freely, without expecting anything in return. At the same time, it has shown me the importance of protecting my energy, standing up for what is right, and advocating for myself and others with grace, wisdom, and dignity. Through self-compassion, I've come to forgive my parents for their shortcomings and, perhaps most importantly, to forgive myself for the anger and resentment I once carried. I now see that my parents were doing the best they could in a world that wasn't built for them, where support for people like us was hard to come by. Their struggles became my inheritance, but so too did the wisdom to rise above those challenges.

As men, we carry a responsibility to dismantle the patriarchy, restore the balance within our families, and honor women as equals in all aspects of life. Compassion requires us to confront both historical and modern-day oppression, recognizing the deep wounds they cause—wounds that make so many feel unworthy, invisible, or powerless. True compassion meets people where they are, without judgment, and this is why self-compassion is so essential. It allows us to extend that same grace to others, to see them not as flawed but as human, navigating their own struggles.

I began my journey into compassion because I was drowning in depression. There were days when the weight of fatherhood, marriage, and life itself felt like too much to bear. I didn't know how to show up for myself, much less for my loved ones. But as I began to cultivate compassion, I realized that those dark days were not my enemies—they were my teachers. They revealed the areas where I needed to grow, where I needed to be kinder to myself, and how I could use my voice and my art as tools for healing, not just for me but for others who shared the same struggles.

The choice to live a compassionate life is always ours to make. Many people choose a different path—one of greed, power, and status. But that road inevitably leads to suffering. Self-compassion allows us to reclaim the parts of ourselves that have been buried under shame, pain, and societal conditioning. It teaches us to let go of the narratives that no longer serve us and to live authentically, in alignment with our values. Real happiness doesn't come from chasing wealth or status—it comes from loving ourselves and others unconditionally and from finding peace in our shared humanity.

Compassion has shown me the profound interconnectedness between all of us. When we heal ourselves, we heal the world around us. This truth became clear to me in the small moments—like when I tend to my garden. As I care for the lemongrass, squash, limes, and tomatoes, I'm reminded of the lessons my grandmother taught me. Watching these plants grow fills me with peace, a deep knowing that love, care, and attention can help not just gardens but people bloom. It reminds me that everything we nurture—whether it's a plant, a relationship, or our own hearts—thrives when we give it our best.

So how can compassion help you be a better version of yourself? A better partner, a better parent, sibling, friend, or even a better steward of the earth? How can it guide you to be kinder not just to others but to yourself? These are the questions that compassion asks of us every day.

CHAPTER 25:

WISE SOULS

"We need leaders not in love with money but in love with justice. Not in love with publicity but in love with humanity."

—Dr. Martin Luther King Jr.

Dr. Gabor Maté suggests that to truly help those who have suffered adverse experiences like the ones discussed in this book, we must allow them to reconnect with who they are at their core. Healing is not about becoming something new but about rediscovering who we were before trauma and shame taught us to loathe ourselves. Dr. Maté explains that trauma stems from a loss of connection to self, often happening in childhood. The path to healing begins with restoring that connection, with rediscovering our true selves. Don Miguel Ruiz, in *The Four Agreements* , speaks of domestication—the way society conditions us, like animals, punishing us for not conforming to expectations. Those of us who have suffered trauma often experience this domestication harshly, punished for feelings or behaviors that stem from our pain. Over time, we begin punishing ourselves, internalizing society's judgment and adopting a narrative of self-hatred.

This domestication begins at home and is reinforced by schools and society at large. I remember when I changed my name from Felipe to Phillip, trying to fit into a world that didn't accept me as I was. That name change represented more than just an attempt to assimilate; it symbolized the shame I felt for being who I truly was. Society taught me that being myself would never be enough, that I had to sacrifice my identity to survive. It wasn't until years later, through self-reflection and the teachings of Dr. Siri, that I realized the depths of the pain I carried. The voice in my head had been shaped by others' expectations, judgments, and punishments, drowning out my true self. Rediscovering who I am has been a process of undoing those negative beliefs and reconnecting with my authenticity.

For those of us who have experienced trauma, the critical work is recognizing the internal voice that has been shaped by the world around us and beginning the process of healing. It is about rejecting the shame and judgment that has been placed upon us and reconnecting with our inherent worth. People who come from backgrounds like mine need hope, inspiration, and examples of resilience from those who have lived through the same challenges. We need leaders who understand the systemic and historical forces that create trauma and who offer compassionate approaches rather than punishment.

As Dr. Bessel van der Kolk teaches, trauma changes the brain, putting people in a constant state of hypervigilance. For many of us, this chronic anxiety shapes every interaction, making us feel judged, unsafe, or rejected in even the simplest situations. This is why mindfulness, self-compassion, and the process of reconnecting with our authentic selves are so vital. These practices can help release the anger, hurt, and pain that keep us stuck in cycles of suffering.

By practicing self-compassion, we can begin to loosen the grip of past trauma, changing our internal dialogue and freeing ourselves from the negative thoughts that have held us captive for so long. Through mindfulness, exercise, and connection with others, we can create new habits and build the life we want. Healing trauma is not a destination but a lifelong journey, one that requires ongoing work, patience, and love.

""The one who plants trees, knowing that he or she will never sit in the shade, has at least started to learn the meaning of life."
—Rabindranath Tagore

Whether this book helps you or someone you know, I hope it opens your heart to a deeper understanding of what it means to live with trauma. In honor of David and Sammy, this journey to compassion is meant to create space for "Wise Souls"—a place where those of us who have experienced trauma can heal and grow through practices like meditation, art, movement, and cultural traditions. As a principal in a school located in one of the poorest areas in the country, I've seen firsthand how compassion can transform lives. I've lived it myself.

On the path of a Wise Soul, we must face misery and suffering head-on, transforming that pain into love and justice for ourselves and others. This journey requires us to reject the conditioned ways of thinking that perpetuate cycles of trauma, rediscover our authenticity, and share our wisdom with the world unapologetically.

As you continue on your own journey, remember: standing firm in the face of pain and embracing compassion is an act of courage and resilience. The love, wisdom, and discipline we cultivate can inspire others, and together, we can create a world that values healing, justice, and love above all.

CHAPTER 26:

STAND FIRM, BE EPIC

"Freedom lies in the first step of your existence."
—Jiddu Krishnamurti

———

Comfort, happiness, and strength lie within you. When you begin to quiet the negative thoughts that once filled your mind, you create space for love and compassion. This is where true wisdom resides. It's not where we start in life, but where we end that defines our journey. As Nipsey Hussle said, "Life is a marathon, not a race." For those of us living with the impact of Poverty 4x, we know the struggle is real. It's important to remember that countless others around the world are enduring their own battles—wars, displacement, oppression. But through it all, learning to love ourselves and embracing emotional agility can transform our suffering into resilience and wisdom.

To stand firm and be epic means understanding that the challenges of Poverty 4x shape how we see ourselves and the world. But it also means knowing we have the power to overcome. When we share our stories, we empower others to love themselves, to reflect on their own reactions with compassion, and to rise above the pain that has weighed them down.

People who endure Poverty 4x often face concentrated suffering from an early age. Without compassionate interventions, that suffering can erode the spirit. But by embracing mindfulness, understanding the neuroscience of trauma, and acknowledging the systemic nature of our struggles, we can begin to heal. We can support one another on this journey, transforming pain into strength and suffering into beauty.

The truth is, people with trauma are not broken. We don't need to be "fixed." What we need are safe spaces where we can be ourselves, express our creativity, and receive positive messages that counter the negative narratives we've lived with for so long. Trauma rewires the brain, but with consistent, loving interventions, we can begin to create new pathways—ones that lead to safety, trust, and healing.

As you move forward, take the first step toward healing by offering yourself and others compassion. Understand that people's behaviors often reflect their suffering, and choose not to carry their pain in your heart. Living with purpose and cultivating compassion is a revolutionary act. It frees you from the shame, hate, and conditioning that have kept you from embracing your true self.

I wrote this book to share my story, to show that no matter where you start, it is possible to rise above pain and suffering. By making changes in our own lives, we can inspire others and help create a world where compassion is the norm—regardless of race, background, or circumstance.

Each chapter is a reflection of my journey—my struggles, my insights, my growth. My hope is that as you read this, you find ways to bring more compassion into your life, to free yourself from the negativity and experiences that have held you back. I believe that by creating environments that support healing rather than punishment, we help people become their true selves—not who society has told them to be.

By exposing more people to the realities of Poverty 4x, we can inspire leaders in these communities—business owners, doctors, lawyers, professors, and professionals—who have grown up in similar conditions to use their resilience and wisdom to guide the next generation. Their experiences can offer others a path rooted in authenticity, rather than in the disingenuous, hustler mentality that often arises from systemic oppression. As a people, we must work together to build a better future for the next seven generations. This involves undoing the intergenerational trauma that has disconnected us as a collective race. It's our duty and obligation to reclaim the traditions, languages, and identities that our ancestors were forced to surrender. They did everything they could to prepare us for a world that stripped so much from them—now it's our time to reclaim our narrative and move forward with strength.

As we look toward the future, let's remember the Ojibwa prayer to help us remember our journey to compassion:

"Teach us love, compassion, and honor that we may heal the earth and each other."
—Ojibwa Prayer

For those striving to break free from the Poverty 4x mindset, begin by journaling at least three times a week. Pay close attention to that inner voice that often dictates your feelings. In this exercise, take a blank sheet of paper and divide it into three columns. In the left column, write down your negative thoughts. In the middle column, reflect on those thoughts—explore where they come from, how they affect your emotions, and how they influence your actions. In the right column, offer yourself a more compassionate perspective.

For example, when negative thoughts arise like, "I am not good enough," or "I don't fit in," write them down. Then ask yourself: Where are these thoughts rooted? How do they cause me to react—anger, shame, self-doubt? After reflecting, imagine yourself in a peaceful state, fully loving yourself without judgment. Would your advice to yourself change? How would you counsel someone you love facing the same situation? Write this compassionate response in the third column.

This practice is especially powerful for communities of color, where we've often been taught to suppress emotions or "tough it out." Many of us carry not just our own trauma, but that of generations before us. Taking time to reflect and reframe these thoughts allows us to break free from colonial and systemic traps that silence our voices and distort our sense of worth. By acknowledging our pain and offering ourselves kindness, we not only heal ourselves but challenge the narratives that have historically kept us down. Loving ourselves in a world that has tried to erase us is a revolutionary act.

You've endured so much, but the strength you need is already inside you. Imagine replacing that negative voice with one that is strong, nurturing, and believes in you. How might this change the way you react, behave, and make decisions? This practice can transform your life—trust in the process, because you are worth it.

The more you practice grace and love for yourself, the more you'll transform the voice that once held you back. A negative mindset will always keep you stuck, but by changing the tone of your inner voice to one of compassion and positivity, you'll begin to truly see and love your authentic self, no matter what the world says. When you heal that voice, you begin to care for yourself in ways you may never have thought possible. You realize your worth, and how sacred you and we all really are.

When you begin to heal yourself and cultivate the self-compassion necessary to break through the walls of negativity, what remains is something unshakable—a radiant, positive, and powerful presence. This is the space where true fulfillment and mental freedom reside. It's where we all aspire to be—a state of wholeness, where the wounds of the past and the weight of society's expectations no longer define us.

But let's be clear: self-compassion alone cannot dismantle racism or undo the deep-rooted systems of oppression that many of us face. It won't fix the forces that continue to marginalize people of color or take away their power. Yet by understanding this, we can cultivate compassion not just for ourselves, but even for those driven by ego and control. We can use our self-awareness and growth to become smarter, more strategic, and position ourselves to bring about systemic change.

Sharing my story has allowed me to reclaim my authentic self, find purpose, and truly heal. It's helped me forgive my parents and, even more difficult, forgive those who killed my brother. That forgiveness was a battle—one that took everything in me, because the anger and pain led me to dark places, making me do and think things I'm not proud of. But through this journey, I've come to see the oppressive forces that shaped our lives, and in understanding that, I found the strength to love deeply—love myself, my family, my people, and my race.

This love didn't just heal my heart; it gave me the courage to imagine a better world and the determination to fight for it. Not with hate or anger, which only fed my suffering, but with compassion and unshakable resolve. It's this transformation, this shift from rage to love, that has empowered me to stand firm, to rise above the hurt, and to turn my pain into purpose.

My deepest hope for humanity is that we all rise to this challenge—that we choose, every day, to create compassionate spaces within ourselves, for those we love, and for the world we share. Healing is a personal journey, but it's also a collective one. The time to heal is now, and the transformation we seek begins within us. Together, we can build a world where love, resilience, and compassion guide us forward, where we use our wisdom to dismantle the structures that hold us back.

This is the space where healing begins, and where love flourishes—not just for yourself, but for others and for the world around you. It's a place where you can exist fully, without apology, without shame, and without fear.

"Just imagine becoming the way you used to be as a very young child, before you understood the meaning of any word, before opinions took over the mind. The real you is loving, joyful, and free. The real you is like a flower, just like the wind, just like the ocean, just like the sun."

—Don Miguel Ruiz

————————

AUTHOR'S NOTES:

I want to honor the Indigenous land we stand on and acknowledge the wisdom, contributions, and sacrifices of our ancestors. Their blood and resilience allow us to be here today, despite all the suffering. Thank you for taking the time to join me on this transformative journey.

As Assata Shakur said, "We need to be weapons of mass construction, weapons of mass LOVE." We can no longer blame individuals without addressing the environments that breed these conditions. We must lead with unconditional love, especially for those who need it most. It's not enough to change the system; we must also change ourselves and how we view children and youth from Poverty 4x.

This journey begins with self-compassion. When we learn to be kind to ourselves, forgive the burdens that don't belong to us, and embrace who we truly are, healing begins. From there, self-compassion blossoms into compassion for others, creating a ripple effect that transforms the spaces we inhabit. Through this transformation, we can support those who need it most and break free from the colonial traps that punish humans for simply surviving in a world that has historically rejected them and their families, forcing assimilation.

ACKNOWLEDGEMENTS

This book is dedicated to my abuelo and abuela, who taught me how to survive, how to be one with myself, and how to honor the earth and our fellow humans. To my Abuelo Pascual Juarez, who was a curandero and healer, I offer my deepest gratitude for providing the foundation that allowed me to seguir adelante (continue forward). My path to compassion and the journey of reflecting on my trauma, my conditioning, and my connection to my roots would not have been possible without his teachings.

With my whole heart and soul, I honor the lives of my brothers, Sammy Mercado and David Vera, whose spirits remind me to stand firm and be epic in everything I do. Most of all, I am grateful for their love, which they gave me before I even knew who I was. Jose Guzman, who taught me how the world works, reminded me that every day is a blessing. Rest in peace to those who lost their lives too soon: Ray Ruiz Jr., Anthony Padilla, Andy Yost, Randy "Stoke" Rios, and Caleb De La Cerda. We must change the narrative for our gente, folx, and ancestors.

To Marissa Betancourt, you saved my life. I met you when I was twelve, and you showed me the power of compassion and its healing strength. When I was homeless and had nothing, you loved me without hesitation. I can never thank you enough. My children, Leilah and Santana Mercado, who endured time without me as I chased my goals and dreams, are resilient souls who teach me daily what it means to be human and what true love feels like. Leilah, Santana, and Marissa (the mother of my children), thank you for loving me unconditionally through it all.

I also offer my deepest appreciation to my mother, Diana Juarez, and my abuela, Edenina Juarez. Despite the suffering that created a barrier between us for much of my life, I honor the struggle you endured for me to be here. I love you both. My brother, Enrique Mercado, has been with me through everything. I love you, bro!

To Sylvia Betancourt-Garza and Virgil Garza, for your unwavering support. To Lorenzo, Lupe, Lulu, and Cindy Betancourt, thank you for always making family gatherings fun and for being there when we needed you most. To the Vera family—Osvaldo (Pap), Fave, and Tencha—for showing me what family truly means. To Carmen Zuniga and Robert Penalber, who gave me a home when I had nothing, and to everyone who offered me a place to stay, whether for a night or a few hours, from ages twelve to nineteen—you will always be in my heart. To Prince Marshall, thank you for helping me grow into my authentic self and for always looking out for me as the big brother I never had. Gordon Jackson, thank you for being the father I never had and showing me how to love like a real man.

To Drs. Nancy Delich and Anne Petrovich, for all your hard work in helping me express this message and your belief in my ability to teach human kindness. To Ellis Vance, for your friendship and humanness. To Drs. Kris Clarke, Christina Luna, and Virginia Hernandez, thank you for always showing me what I can offer the world and that there is space for me. Dr. Ken Magdaleno, for helping me understand how to give back to my people. To Christian Wandeler, Frank Carbajal, Jackie Camacho Ruiz, Izar Olivares, and Robert Pimentel, thank you for supporting me on my journey and for being unique beings and beams of light. Jerry Tello and Alberto Herrera, thank you for teaching me about my cultura and for accepting me as I was and am, as my uncles. Leena Mendoza, thank you for believing in me and pushing me to become something greater than I ever imagined. Dr. Siri Sat Nam, thank you for your mentorship and for helping me heal my inner child. Erika Rosenberg, Lakiba Pittman, and Ashley Potvin, along with the Compassion Institute, Center for Compassion Leadership, and the World Happiness Academy, thank you for supporting me on my compassion journey.

Lastly, and most importantly, thank you to all of you who will work to change our world. Together, we can create a more compassionate future—one where we heal, not lead from trauma, ego, or greed. In a world where everyone is accepted for who they are, our diversity will become the driving force behind the innovation and sustainability we need to preserve our race and heal our earth.

ABOUT THE AUTHOR

Dr. Felipe Mercado, Ed.D, MSW, PPSC, is a Professor at California State University, Fresno, in the Social Work Department and the founder of Wise Soul LLC. He has previously been an elementary school principal, university and district coordinator, K-8 deputy principal, vice principal, counselor, social worker, cultural broker, public speaker, educational consultant, curriculum designer, prison instructor, and researcher/ program evaluator.

Over the past decade, Felipe has worked to facilitate trauma healing circles and restorative mediations, compassionate meditations, keynote speeches, curriculum design, leadership development, and scientific lectures for districts, community colleges, universities, nonprofits, and the private sector. Felipe is a Certified Compassion Cultivation Teacher with the Compassion Institute and Mindfulness and Happiness Coach with The World Happiness Academy.

His training and experiences in Dare 2 Lead, Emotional Intelligence, Trauma Informed Healing, Compassionate Leadership, Social Work, Counseling, Education, and Administration support Felipe in bringing the pedagogy from theory to practice and blending best practices from these disciplines to create new and innovative ways of being human together and be productive. Dr. Siri Sat Nam has mentored Dr. Mercado. During this experience, Felipe learned mastery of the self, how to heal using compassion, and found his purpose in life.

Felipe received the CSU, Fresno Health and Human Services "Community Hero" award in 2019. His company Wise Soul LLC seeks to support humans and organizations through evidence-based approaches rooted in neuroscience, neurobiology, and organizational psychology to promote compassionate, productive, and happier spaces.

Felipe Mercado, E.D., MSW, PPSC
Wisesouls.com
LinkedIn: @Felipe Mercado Ed.D.
IG: @dr.mercado.ws

Made in the USA
Las Vegas, NV
02 December 2024

13198748R00118